REBEL BRASS
The Confederate Command System

REBEL BRASS

The Confederate Commana System

By FRANK E. VANDIVER

Introduction by T. *HARRY WILLIAMS*

GREENWOOD PRESS, PUBLISHERS
NEW YORK

For

Mom and Dad

and for

Boone Atkinson, Harvey Gardiner, and Harry Williams

Foreword

THROUGHOUT THE YEARS of its existence, the Confederacy was caught up in a massive war effort which finally touched all elements of life in the South. It was a new sort of national war, for which the South (as well as the North) was unprepared. While campaigning to sustain the rights of the states, the Confederate government found itself forced to increased war controls and harsh centralization. This curious situation posed new problems, the most fundamental of which was perhaps one of method. How is such a total war managed? What sort of direction is needed and how is it achieved?

The objective in the following pages is to discuss the direction of this Confederate war effort—but to discuss it in a special way. "Direction" in this case is to be looked upon as a command function. The term "command," for the purposes of this book, is used in the broadest sense. Its meaning is not to be restricted simply to the wielding of authority by military leaders—although this is certainly included. Rather, it will be used to discuss the direction of the whole Southern war effort,

REBEL BRASS

which is to say it will include all echelons of leadership—civil as well as military. Two of the major
questions raised, and I fear not completely an-
swered, are: Was the Confederate command system adequate to the job of fighting the Civil War?
Did the Confederacy fail because command failed?

The task of examining Southern high command
in full detail (which would be necessary to answer
these two questions) is too large to be accomplished
in a small volume. Consequently, limits have been
set—limits which make possible only an introduction to the subject. Command is viewed from but
three avenues: first, as a national problem; second,
as it was understood and practiced by civilian leaders; third, as it affected the whole area of logistics.

Logistics, that complicated process of supplying
armies, is included because it represents the area
where integrated direction—both civilian and military—was most needed. The management of logistical operations often was confused and lacked
co-ordination. An attempt will be made to offer
some possible reasons for these deficiencies and to
show their effects.

I should emphasize the point that this book does
not attempt a definitive study of command and its
influence during the war. By treating restricted
parts of the Confederate story, the book is aimed at
opening a new area for future research—an area
in which there is room aplenty for work.

Too much of a case may be made for the importance of command in these pages, but command is used as an approach to an over-all pattern for Confederate history. Since the present treatment is not by any means complete, I hope allowances will be made. I hope, too, that the idea may draw the criticism of Civil War students—for if interest enough is created to produce criticism it has served its purpose.

I would like to acknowledge with thanks the many convivial evenings of conversation at "Lincolnand" with Dr. and Mrs. T. Harry Williams and my wife Susie. It was during one of our caustic (but bloodless) arguments about "The War" that the original scheme for this book was hatched.

Thanks are equally due to Dr. Frank L. Owsley, of the University of Alabama, Dr. Joseph G. Tregle, Jr., of Loyola University in New Orleans, and Dr. C. Harvey Gardiner, of Washington University in St. Louis, for reading the manuscript and offering valuable criticisms and suggestions for improvement. My cousin, Major Perry Craddock, U.S.A., also read the manuscript and suggested some important additions. My father-in-law, Mr. Alex P. Smith, of Dallas, read the first draft. His wealth of experience in the field of logistics strengthened some shaky passages.

FRANK E. VANDIVER
Department of History
The Rice Institute

September, 1955

[ix]

Contents

Illustrations

Introduction

IN *Lincoln Reconsidered*—a recent pene-
trating study of America's most-studied war—Professor David Donald ventures the opinion that the
amount, the tremendous amount, of Civil War literature is adequate for present scholarly needs. Our
generation, he states, is not likely to witness major
discoveries of new facts or fresh sources. Contem-
plating the massive aggregation of source and sec-
ondary works now in print, Donald doubts that
further investigation of familiar themes is necessary or that continued efforts to unearth additional
knowledge will serve any useful purpose. We have
reached a point, he thinks, where scholars of the
war must change their emphasis. They "will have
to concentrate less upon uncovering some long-
forgotten body of manuscripts and more upon re-
thinking the basic issues. . . . Unless Civil War
historiography degenerates into antiquarianism,
with more and more elaborate biographies being
written about less and less significant minor char-
acters, we must turn to fresh problems and to fresh
solutions of old problems. . . ."

Mr. Donald's notion that Civil War scholarship

has searched out, at least for the present, sufficient facts and that research, at least in the immediate future, should grind to a halt is certain to shock that most dedicated of all reading groups in the nation, the ever-growing body of Civil War buffs. It should be taken, as he probably meant it to be, with a large reservation. Nevertheless, his suggestion—perhaps counsel is an apter word—that scholars should shift their emphasis is essentially sound and is based upon a thorough appreciation of the nature of Civil War historiography. The writers who have compiled and produced the literature of America's favorite war have been primarily interested in bringing to light new documents and fresh facts. They have not neglected interpretation or synthesis—indeed, on these counts their work compares favorably with the efforts of writers in all other fields of American history—but there has been an undeniable sense of urgency, a kind of relentless drive, to discover the unknown. Now the time has undoubtedly come to stop and take stock, to evaluate what we have, to rethink the meaning of the vast knowledge we possess.

A job of thinking is what Professor Frank E. Vandiver undertakes in *Rebel Brass,* thinking based on the findings of previous scholars and on his own considerable research. He has chosen to describe and analyze a spacious subject—the Confederate high command, the men who composed it, the decisions they made, and the influences which shaped their policy. In modern war, which is total and all-embracing, the factor of command is of overriding importance. The verdicts decided upon at the highest level of command may determine whether a nation wins or loses, lives or dies. The Civil War was the first of the modern wars, and the command systems established by both sides are a vital part of the war story. The nature of those systems helps to explain the outcome of the struggle.

In Mr. Vandiver's pages we receive a concise description of the machinery of the Confederate high command. We get something more—a sharp analysis of the human personalities who dominated the system. The portraits drawn here of Jefferson Davis and of Secretaries Randolph, Seddon, and Mallory are among the best sketches we have of Confederate leaders. They may seem harsh to some readers, but the seemingly acid quality does not proceed from any animus or prejudice on the part of the author. Rather, it is the result of his profound conviction that the men who guided the destinies of the Confederacy were the victims of a system which they had helped to create and which they were trying to sustain by methods that could never succeed. In all the long history of war there is probably no better illustration than the Confederacy of the truth of Clausewitz' dictum that a nation will fight a war that resembles its social system. The Southern nation was founded on the principle of state rights, and localism controlled—and impeded—the way it waged war, the strategic thinking of its chieftains, and its efforts to form an efficient command system. In the groping and sometimes pathetic attempts of President Davis to move toward a tighter command arrangement, we see a man caught in a grim historical trap. It is one of the great contributions of Professor Vandiver's study that he recognizes the impact of Southern culture upon Confederate warmaking. Although this is primarily a work of dissection rather than of narrative, it conveys as vividly as any biography of Lee or any history of the embattled South the mood of impending and inevitable doom that hung over the Southern adventure in independence. There are elements of high tragedy in this book—and some military lessons that all students of war would do well to ponder.

It may be said by some that Mr. Vandiver, now thirty years of age, is too young a scholar to be pontificating about the nature of Confederate command arrangements or the causes of Southern defeat, that such weighty issues should be left to the elder statesmen in the field. Even if years of sustained research constituted the sole qualification to generalize— which is not necessarily the case—Mr. Vandiver meets the test. In terms of actual time of service the youthful professor is a seasoned veteran. Civil War scholars have a certain fanatic quality about them, but even among this determined band who live most of their waking hours in the 1860's Mr. Vandiver holds a unique place. He published his first schol-

[xvi]

arly article on the war when he was sixteen and has been turning out essays and books ever since. His opinions, then, are the result of years of study and reflection, and they represent a much greater maturity of scholarship than his age would seem to indicate. Most of Mr. Vandiver's investigations have been in an area which he has made peculiarly his own and in which he has attained the rank of an authority—logistics, the science of supplying armies with needed matériel at the right time and in the right place. Not the least of the many contributions of *Rebel Brass* is the author's brilliant exposition of the influence of logistics upon Southern command problems. Undoubtedly some of his ranging generalizations concerning the Confederate high command will arouse dissent; probably some are wrong. And possibly in the future he himself may wish to modify a few of them. But readers of this book will miss its point and lose its value if they view it as a polemical work, as an item to be argued about. It is not a systematic or exhaustive treatment of either the high command or Southern strategy. It is the first attempt to examine the bases of Confederate strategic thinking, and it should stimulate other scholars to think about the function of command and to study the story of the strategy of the Confederacy, thereby casting new illumination on why the Lost Cause was lost. *Rebel Brass* is, then, to use an over-used phrase, both an end and a beginning.

T. HARRY WILLIAMS

CHAPTER ONE

Total War and the Problem of Command

THERE WAS SOMETHING intangibly different about the Civil War. The difference was not immediately apparent to those running it or to those fighting it. When the war began in 1861 it seemed as though it would be like most wars—possibly just a little bigger. It was with the passage of time that the changes became apparent. The war made its own innovations, and the men responsible for directing it on both sides had to evolve new methods of leadership and new ideas of command.

Confederate leaders in 1861 had certain well-established notions of how to wage war. These notions came from previous American wars, and no one bothered to re-examine military doctrine to see if anything had changed. The officials struggling to create all branches of a government for the Confederate States of America had neither the time nor the sense of urgency to go deeply into the nature of war. They approached the initial problems of military organization with old techniques and

[3]

old concepts of military science. Most of these men had no idea that a war, if it came, would last very long. It is not surprising, therefore, that in the early months of 1861 the changing character of warfare went unrecognized by the Confederates.

Thinking in terms of the Mexican War, a half-generation earlier, both the North and South went about preparing their land and naval forces in the traditional manner. The command of divisions and flotillas was handled on a highly informal, individual basis. Previous wars had been run on an essentially personal plane, with individual generals fighting individual campaigns, and with minimal direction from Washington. This is the way it was to be in the Confederacy. No thought, at first, was given to the creation of a centralized agency in the capital charged with any sort of unification of military operations or with unifying the civil and military war efforts. Actually, the idea of a civilian war effort was unfamiliar to all but a few Confederate leaders.

What unity of effort there was would naturally come from the President, the Secretary of War, and the Secretary of the Navy. Tradition was the guide; these offices had sufficed in the past—why not in 1861? Supposedly, experience was the best of teachers and the warmakers of 1861 could hardly be expected to scrap the lessons learned in previous conflicts.

The influence of the past was reflected in the

composition of the military and naval departments of the Confederate States. The War Secretary, under the President, was charged with the direction of the armies of the South. Under the Secretary of War there were certain staff departments which had grown up in the United States during the course of years: the Quartermaster General's Office, the Surgeon General's Office, and a few others. The heads of these agencies were responsible to the secretary, as were the commanders of the various field forces. It would be the job of the secretary to co-ordinate the operations of the field and staff commands. The same sort of arrangement prevailed in the Navy Department, where similar staff departments were responsible to the cabinet officer, who in turn furnished what unity of effort existed. This organization had worked fairly well in the days when armies were smaller, but time, changing many things, demanded changes in the system of command.

By sticking closely to tradition in 1861, the North and South made some early mistakes—mistakes which the North overcame with a new command system in 1864. Southern leaders tried to create a modern command system also, but numerous factors prevented complete success.

Since there was nothing in the Confederate command structure in the beginning which could be construed as restricting the authority of the states to organize their own military units for state defense (nor could there have been because of state rights), state operations soon came into conflict with Confederate mobilization plans. Initial organization was seriously hampered by too many different enterprises going on at once. The end result was fragmentary mobilization, confusion, and much wasted effort. Not only were men put into the field as state militia units and as Confederate forces, but the rather loose approach to military administration resulted in serious complications in clothing and equipping the troops. States wanted to care for their own men and no others. The Confederate government, desperate to get some men into the field, was forced to accept with thanks all the efforts of the various states and to try to work out the questions of state and national authority later. The attempt to bypass the issue may have seemed like a good idea at first, but the problem was so serious that it was never solved.

Born partially out of protest against centralization of federal power, the Confederate government wanted to stand as a model of decentralization and as a bulwark for state sovereignty. Frank L. Owsley, in *State Rights in the Confederacy,* has observed that the South had the seeds of death implanted at birth and that the seeds were those of state rights. The doctrine of the supremacy of the states went far toward retarding any sort of unification of the Confederate war effort—possibly making the Confederacy a good example of Clausewitz' dictum that a nation will fight a war like its own political system.

•A central agency charged with planning Confederate mobilization—a general staff—might have minimized some of the bad effects of "separate state action."• Such a staff might have channeled men and supplies where most needed and might have prevented the piling up of equipment for some troops while others, in remote areas, had absolutely nothing.•

It is possible that such an agency (unprecedented in American military history up to that time) could have performed an even more valuable service for the Confederacy by giving direction and some semblance of uniformity to the question of strategy. •One of the first questions involving strategy which plagued the Confederate government would have been logically the province of such an organization: Where were the Confederate military frontiers? How far north should the South try to hold the line? At least one officer not directly concerned with strategic planning gave some thought to this and felt that it merited more attention. Major Josiah Gorgas, the able Chief of Ordnance, wanted some decision reached on Confederate strategy so that he would know how to distribute his munitions supply. No uniformity of strategic thinking was achieved. The command problem was much larger than it appeared on the surface and this reduced the possibility of achieving unity in a short time—if at all.

At least six major factors complicated the command picture: (1) the geographical pattern of the Confederate States, (2) manpower, (3) leadership, (4) economy, (5) Southern attitude toward the war, and (6) communications.

Looking at the new nation on a map, the peculiar physical location of its presumed borders was easily seen. Surrounded by a tremendous coastline on the east and south and by hostile, or potentially neutral, states to the west and north, the Confederacy was cut by several large rivers. This geographical situation was clearly related to the over-all military strategy of the South.

The coastline could be a tremendous asset. The numerous small inlets, roadsteads, and harbors furnished ample facilities for shipping. Shipping could mean trade to bolster the South's economy and could also bring in war supplies from abroad which would make up for some of the nation's industrial weakness. And the coastline was so large that should the United States Navy attempt a blockade, the task would be virtually impossible—even without a large Confederate Navy to oppose the Federal fleet.

The lay of the Confederate land from Texas to Virginia gave an apparent strategiçal advantage. The South seemingly would be able to wage war on inner lines of communication—a strategist's dream. This meant that in normal circumstances the Confederates would find it easier to move men and supplies from one part of their territory to another than would the North. This advantage was perhaps more fanciful than real, since the North frequently had this same opportunity as the war progressed.

Inner lines would be even more of a fiction unless the Confederate transportation network could sustain operations stretching across tremendous distances. Since, in the early stages of the fighting, it did not appear that campaigns would spread too far afield, not many people worried about transportation. But times changed, and distance was to become a backbreaking curse of Southern military operations as railroads deteriorated.

The mountain ranges which penetrated the South in Virginia and in Tennessee were not an unmixed blessing. While some Confederate commanders were able to use mountains to screen their operations, so were some of the Union generals. As time passed, the mountains, plus the distances involved, served to reduce the efficiency of command. They tended, in some instances, to isolate the Secretary of War in Richmond. The rivers, leading into the South at many points, were even more of a hazard.

• The most obvious route for bisecting the Confederacy was the Mississippi. If that were taken by the Union, other rivers might be used to splinter

[9]

the country further. The Cumberland, Tennessee, James, York, Ocmulgee, Cape Fear, and the Red were all possible invasion routes. The Confederate Navy, with some help from the army and the Marine Corps, would have to stop such incursions if possible.

For various reasons, then, geography offered both strength and weakness to the Confederate war effort.

Manpower was another factor in command. The war could not be fought without fighting men. Other factors had their importance, but none was so fundamental as manpower. Here the South felt rich enough. All Southerners knew that the Southern people were of a more martial spirit than their Northern enemies. Any fear of a scarcity of soldiers was dissipated by the fact that the army had to turn down over two hundred thousand volunteers in 1861 because there were no arms available with which to equip them. (It was assumed, of course, that the men would still be there when the arms were found.) Nor were Southerners worried by cold statistics showing that the population of the North vastly outnumbered them, for any Southern soldier could whip ten Yankees.

These were mistakenly optimistic ideas. War was no longer confined to armies. It had taken on grimmer overtones of factories and industrial potential and economics. Manpower involved not only soldiers in the field, but skilled workers in the

munitions and clothing factories and in the shipyards. The Confederate war effort was seriously
crippled by the fact that the new dimension of
manpower was not yet clear. Never during the war
was an adequate policy evolved for handling the
relatively few skilled workers in the South. More
and more of them were taken into the ranks, with a
direct inverse effect on war production. •

In a strong bid to keep up the armies, the South
resorted to conscription in 1862. The Bureau of
Conscription was not efficiently managed and,
faced with spreading resistance to the increased
governmental authority, did a poor job of drafting
men. This agency was abolished in 1865, after Congress and the President became convinced it was
keeping more men at home than it was putting in
uniform.

In the final analysis, despite Confederate feelings
to the contrary, there were not enough men. As
attrition, along with desertion, took more men from
the ranks, replacements could not be found. The
manpower factor alone did not lose the war for the
Confederacy, but combined with poor policies re-
sulting in the misuse of this resource, manpower
failed to sustain the war.

A third factor in the command problem was the
human element of leadership. This was, of course,
the most intangible of all factors. Here, though, the
South felt it had a real asset. As far as military
talent was concerned, the Confederacy had some of

the best that was available. A number of West Point–trained officers cast their lot with the South; some resigned their commissions in the United States Army, others volunteered from civil life. Many of these officers had military experience in the Mexican War. Men like Lee, the two Johnstons, Stonewall Jackson, and Jeb Stuart were among the best that West Point could offer. Nor were trained naval officers lacking, for serving the Confederacy were such men as Franklin Buchanan, Raphael Semmes, and Josiah Tattnall, among others.

Ordinarily, talent of such an impressive nature would serve to overbalance a lot of shortcomings. This was, to some extent, true in the Confederacy. These men did wonders with the limited material at hand. But there is a reverse side to the coin. The possibility exists that the "professional" officer brought with him the old concepts of war he learned in school and in Mexico, and that he was slower than many untrained men to see war as a changed business. Nathan Bedford Forrest, who was militarily untutored but fought a modern type of war, might illustrate the point.

Manpower was an economic problem as well as a human one. It was one of the natural resources of the South. As such, it is part of the fourth factor confounding the command picture: economy. The economic structure of the South was unable to support a long war. Money was the basic problem, for there was simply not enough. Foreign trade and markets were cut off by the blockade. The natural resources needed for a prolonged effort were available, to some extent, but many were unknown or unexploited. The economy probably could have maintained a short war, but the fact that the South organized and propped up a large military effort for four years largely based on the agricultural system of 1861 is a tribute to the ingenuity of the Confederates.

As the war dragged on, more sources of war materiel had to be found. Lead, iron, steel, tin, zinc, copper, niter, sulphur, leather, paper, rubber, oil, salt, coffee, medicines, rope, glue, and many other essentials all ran short. Where could additional supplies be found?

These necessities were never in adequate supply (possibly excepting iron and copper), which proportionately reduced the efficiency of the Confederate effort. Little was known about the sources of these items—mineral resources, for instance—at the beginning of the war. They had to be found by trial and error.

Exploiting natural resources posed a large problem, particularly in view of how little was known in the South about the use of such factors in a total war effort.

On the surface the Confederacy was not so materially weak as the recitation of shortages indicates. In addition to the limited, possibly fictional, advantage given by inner lines, the South had ample agricultural resources for a long war. There would be no food shortage, or so reason indicated. Cotton existed in abundance, and since Europe needed the commodity constantly, the South should be able to bank on a continuous supply of capital. These two strengths were weakened by poor economic and diplomatic policies which allowed them to be frittered away piecemeal.

Southern economy had been relatively healthy in 1860—healthy enough, some Southerners thought, to exist as a separate entity. Southern leaders had been preaching the South's self-sufficiency for years. Such a course could only be successful, though, in an atmosphere of peace, where the heavy emphasis of the Southern economy toward agriculture could have been offset by foreign manufactured goods. In a wartime situation, with restricted trade, the material weaknesses of the section were crushing.

There was one significant iron foundry in the whole Confederacy in 1861, which meant that heavy ordnance and railroad equipment could be made in only one place. All the industrial strength of the old United States lay to the north of Mason and Dixon's line. There were a few scattered machine shops and factories in the South, but nothing to compare with the North. The same was true of shipbuilding facilities. The only yard capable of heavy work was at Norfolk, Virginia. Without more of the same, a real Confederate Navy could never float.

As the war continued, a few more ironworks were developed, including some rolling mills, and limited railroad-repair shops were erected. These shops were confined largely to Virginia, Georgia, and Alabama. Shipbuilding never flourished. Ordnance plants were put into successful operation in Virginia, North Carolina, Georgia, and Alabama, but most of them needed more and better machinery.

These material weaknesses had a direct influence on Confederate strategy. Since the few industrial areas of the South were fairly well concentrated along the eastern seaboard (with the exceptions of Selma, Alabama, and San Antonio, Texas), the problem of getting raw materials to the plants and finished products to depots and armies was urgent. Much depended on the railroads, which deteriorated rapidly as repair facilities dwindled. Then, too, the lines close to the Atlantic coast or the northern frontiers were easily subject to enemy attack. The failing transportation lines dictated a decentralization of industrial facilities, but this often was impossible. Consequently, it became extremely important to defend the industrial areas of the South. This tended to fix Confederate military policy toward a war of position. The weak transportation network retarded, to some degree, the freedom of movement of the Confederate armies.•

The fact that facilities for developing and expanding Southern economic resources were scarce also affected military thinking.•Unable to think too far ahead or to count on unlimited war materiel, Confederate leadership became increasingly defensive in its outlook.•

Perhaps the most far-reaching factor in command was the fifth—the Southern outlook on the nature of war. The initial Southern overconfidence (an attitude shared equally by the North) is well known. The war would last no more than ninety days, just long enough to produce some wonders for the Confederates. No one was silly enough to say that the South wanted to fight an aggressive, invasion-type war. This would be a war for separation, not territorial aggrandizement. This rationalization fitted in nicely with the continuing pressure from state and local officials for home defense against Federal invasion. It would be good politics, and by a small stretch of imagination good tactics, to keep the troops close to home.

Such thinking helped create a defensive attitude in the Confederate mind.•A defensive war would also be a war of position, which might lighten the supply problem. Certain vital centers like Richmond would be held at all costs. Once geographical determinism was firmly planted in the minds of

Confederates, they cast off all pretense at the correct strategy of eliminating enemy armies. Wedded irrevocably to ground, they buried themselves in it?

The sixth major command factor was communications. Here, too, old-style military thinking was at first in vogue. Although the era of the electric telegraph had dawned, little reliance was put on this modern convenience in the early stages of the conflict—particularly on the battlefield, where the old courier system was retained. Considerable use was eventually made of the telegraph by the Confederacy, but not nearly so much as by the Union. There were good reasons for this. Telegraph wire was in short supply in the South; in the North it was plentiful. Then, too, there were many more telegraphists in the North than in the South. The Federals used this new method of communication extensively, keeping army headquarters in contact with the action. The Confederates did not do so well. The War Department in Washington was well informed of what was happening all over the war zones. Not so with Richmond and the Confederate War Department. Frequently much time elapsed before reports of a battle could reach a telegraph office. The most original attempt at rapid battlefield communication made by the South was the introduction into the armies of semaphore signals.

Both sides relied heavily on numerous staff officers, in addition to the couriers, to carry dispatches.

Since contact with all the various elements of an army in action or on campaign was so dependent on this highly personalized messenger service, it was natural that field officers were surrounded by large staffs. In the earlier battles the work of these staffs was poorly done. Most of the men had little or no military experience, found it difficult to master their assignments, and wasted a lot of time. A raw, green staff seriously hampered Confederate plans.

In time the Confederate staff service improved. The South moved toward a separate staff corps composed of men with long experience and wisdom in battle. The fact that such a corps was organized by Congress indicates the growing complexity of war, and is an admission that the older system of communication was inadequate. But a general staff, which would have embraced and gone far beyond the functions of the field staff, was never created. Specialization might be a curse in some ways, but a little bit of it lavished on a general staff corps undoubtedly would have been worth the trouble. Better co-ordination of the information which did reach Richmond would have resulted and the armies would have been more efficiently handled.

What combined effect did all these factors have on command? Essentially, they retarded the recognition of command's basic nature. The war, it was soon apparent, was not to be short. The longer it lasted, the more obvious became the weaknesses of the Confederacy. The more these were recognized, the more each branch of the war effort desperately sought to bolster its own position, with little consideration for other branches.

The new Federal "Anaconda" policy, exerting pressure all along the Confederate line, brought out a new concept of war for which the South found itself wholly unprepared. Such total war, in which everybody was a cog in a national war effort, was a surprise. Civilian morale was now as important as soldier morale; civilian resistance as important as military resistance. The need for all types of supplies could only be met by full-scale civilian production. The dream of a Walter Scott South did not die at Appomattox—it died in the furnaces and clothing mills of a maximum war effort. It died when Southern women copied the "wage slaves" of Lowell and made bullets, arms, and uniforms, as well as bandages.

The transition was too much. It came too fast. Jefferson Davis began to see the need of a centralized government to fight the war, but even he was unaware of how far this might have to go. Struggling to fight a national war amid state rights ideas was an impossible task. Total war could not be waged piecemeal.

But it was with a piecemeal approach that the Confederacy departmentalized its effort, not only governmentally, but militarily. Generals of various field forces had to fend for themselves in isolated areas. Richmond, to which all looked for guidance, was the nerve center of the Confederacy, but a nerve center lacking the power of co-ordination. Distances were too great and communications too slow. Various schemes were tried to overcome this estrangement, but none was fully successful.

Gradually, whole areas drifted out of the Richmond orbit. The Trans-Mississippi Department, after the fall of Vicksburg, was to all practical purposes lost. Richmond authorities could never be certain that communications reached this area, and it was so remote from the capital that the government dared not direct operations about which it could know so little.

What happened to the Trans-Mississippi Department happened elsewhere. Bits and dribbles of the manpower reserve were siphoned off here and there to hold first one spot and then another. Eventually, the middle Confederacy—east Louisiana, Mississippi, and Alabama—was under only nominal control from Richmond. The combination of distance and geography resulted in splintering the South.

It seems doubtful that anyone in the Confederate hierarchy understood the real nature of the command problem. Command was a function which could be delegated, but not abdicated, by the government. Everything about a war effort is basically a command problem, and nothing going on in a country is beyond the scope of strategic high command planning. This was certainly true in the Confederacy. If the real nature of the problem had been understood early in the war it would have been clear that there were no isolated actions. No general could be allowed to fend for himself without doing violence to the scheme of the war. War, by the 1860's, had taken on a new aspect. It was now a phenomenon of extensive and rapid movement, which gave rise to a new dimension in the old science of logistics. Mass movements of mass armies and supplies involved the whole economy and all of society. Consequently, everything was a command responsibility. •

Co-ordination is a basic ingredient of high command. The frequent references in contemporary literature to Confederate "armies" are more accurate than they first appear to be. There was no real "Army" during the whole war. The Secretary of War and the Adjutant General did very little to co-ordinate operations. In addition, there was, as usual, practically no co-operation between the army and navy. Both the Secretary of War and the Secretary of the Navy went their own separate ways.

Confederate failure to recognize, in time to make any difference, that war had become a national experience reflects the lack of strategic planning, not a want of foresight. Over-all direction of the Southern war effort was never provided. A general staff might have been the answer, but it was never tried. There is some evidence, however, that as the war progressed the Confederate government began to see the need for some type of comprehensive command. Several experiments were tried in an effort to obtain limited, but still largely local, co-ordination of military operations. Efficient and quick integration of the military and nonmilitary aspects of war was too much to expect of a nation dedicated to decentralization.

CHAPTER TWO

Command and Civilian
Administration

STANDING FIRMLY on fundamental American tradition, the Confederates looked upon the military as thoroughly subordinated to the civil authorities. According to the Constitution the President was the commander in chief of the army and navy, and of the state militia forces when called into Confederate service. Under the President were civilian secretaries presiding directly over the Department of War and the Department of the Navy. Theoretically, these cabinet officers would relieve the President of much annoying detail, thus letting the chief executive devote himself to policy-making and general supervision of military affairs.

Jefferson Davis did things differently. He had certain ideas about army command. These ideas were based partly on his education and experience; partly, it seems, on prejudice. He was well educated academically and militarily. After being graduated from the United States Military Academy in 1828 he soon turned to the soil and became a citizen planter in Mississippi. By most standards he was a material success. A deep personal tragedy drove him to years of seclusion on his plantation, during which time he devoted himself to little else than crops and reading. These years, though, apparently were not lost to the keen intellect of a man of his nature. When he was sent to the national House of Representatives in 1845 he was already steeped in ideas about the relationship of government to the governed. With the coming of the Mexican War, he resigned his seat in the House to take a commission as colonel of a Mississippi regiment. When he returned to Washington in 1847 it was as a senator from Mississippi.

The years between West Point and the Senate changed Davis. His experience as a field officer in Mexico had a lasting effect on his self-estimate. Mexican service seems to have convinced him that he was something of a military expert, not to say genius. He savored the taste of gunpowder for years. As a senator, Davis gave much attention to military affairs, and snapped at the opportunity, in 1853, to serve Franklin Pierce as his Secretary of War.

There was something natural to Davis about the office of Secretary of War. It was as if, somehow, all the intervening time had been preparing him for this. He was qualified as few were for the task. With an understanding of things martial provided by professional training, he was tempered with war service and with the thinking of a civilian agent of the taxpayers. He was expected to do well in Pierce's cabinet, and he did not disappoint the President.

The trouble was that Davis was too good at his job. This fact was the essential ingredient in a great personal tragedy—the tragedy of a man who had a higher duty thrust upon him in future years, but who could never really let go of a more natural job. In the years to come, when the direction of a whole nation's war effort fell to Davis, he was unable to step completely beyond the office of the Secretary of War. A position calling for executive ability and the capacity to delegate authority found him wanting. He could not bring himself to trust others with military trivia. When the times demanded daring, he could only be cautious.

All of which leads to the question: What kind of revolutionary leader was Jefferson Davis? As President of the Confederacy he had to concern himself with strategy; high-level planning was a daily chore. As a strategist Davis probably does not rank with Lincoln, particularly as far as over-all war planning is concerned. Davis took a much narrower, more militarist view of the war that prevented him from seeing many new facets which time had introduced to the art of national assassination.

Davis' strategic thinking grew smaller and smaller, with results in direct ratio to the thoughts.

Circumstances were partly to blame for this. After a while he could see little beyond the confines of Richmond and Lee's military department. For some time Davis limited his concept of strategy almost wholly to field operations and consequently did little with the idea of total war.

To some degree the nature of his task dulled his vision. Out of vast numbers of independent, uncooperative groups he had to try to build unity. This was a dreary, daily business with scant reward. Criticism of everything he did came from everywhere, and as a defensive aloofness settled over him, he removed himself from a realistic connection with the war.

A combination of political pressure and the policy of nonaggression made him stick to defensive thinking. Defense is not an easy task, and one of its most dangerous pitfalls can be loss of initiative. This happened to Davis. Cities and geography became vastly important to him, and he dispersed Confederate forces to hold certain areas. This war of position pinned down troops which might otherwise have been available for the attack.

The fatal mixture of politics, military command, and his personality proved to be Davis' undoing. His belief in himself as a competent field commander inevitably complicated his administrative duties as President. Had he been able to be one or the other, things might have been different. The Constitution helped trap him by making him commander in chief of the army and navy. A strict constitutionalist, he found it difficult to yield any constitutional prerogative. The President was entrusted with military leadership, and he must exercise it. From his point of view, of course, it was fortunate that he had had professional soldierly training. In reality it was an inestimable curse.

Unlike Lincoln, Davis knew the rules of war too well. He could not forget them when occasion demanded. He also knew the Constitution too well, and when the need arose he could not discard the supreme law of the land. The great paradox of the Confederacy was clearly reflected by Davis' dilemma: he was leader of a revolution, and yet he had a legal mind. Revolution and strict legality were somehow incompatible.

One of the prime reasons for the failure of Davis, and of the Confederate cause, was constitutionalism. This was a chronic complaint of the Old South, finally leading to secession as a remedy. Now the remedy killed the patient.

Considered within the limited scope of command which he set for himself, Davis was not a bad leader. He understood the basic organization of armies and was more aware than most other civil officials of the importance of logistics. And let it be said in his favor that Davis was no coward. He was anxious to strike the Yankees whenever possible, and even ignored political pressure to the extent of sanctioning invasion of the North on two occasions. His

[27]

personal foresight and diligence led to the early purchasing abroad of some vitally needed war supplies, which may well have made it possible for the Confederacy to stay in the field for the first year. He was a man of spirit. Defeat could add to his frosty demeanor, but he was a die-hard. Anyone who doubted his personal bravery had only to hear the tragic story of the death of his son in the President's mansion to know that there was something special in this man.

Strong men sometimes have odd weaknesses. One of Davis' strangest was a fierce, almost unreasoning loyalty to his friends. Once Davis took a man into his circle of friends, he was there to stay—no matter what others might say of him or prove about him. For a president this is more than a foible; it may well be a catastrophe. It nearly was. People like the incompetent Commissary General, Lucius B. Northrop, and General Braxton Bragg remained in their posts doing vast damage because they were friends of the President and by definition could do no wrong.

Enemies were enemies, no matter what. The same stubbornness that he showed in loyalty to his friends made it impossible for Davis to forgive an enemy or to see much good in him. This unfortunate predisposition cost the Confederacy the most effective services of General P. G. T. Beauregard, General Joseph E. Johnston, and others.

There were times, though, when Davis tried to

see above personal prejudice for the good of the country. On these occasions he was open to suggestions from trusted advisors, and Secretary of War James A. Seddon seems to have been particularly effective in urging reason over personalities. Despite the well-known distrust, not to say dislike, which the President felt for Johnston and Beauregard, Seddon succeeded in getting Davis to entrust these two men with the largest military commands created within the Confederacy.

Johnston was appointed to the command of the Department of the West in late 1862. He was to give unity of direction to the operations of Bragg's and John C. Pemberton's armies. Johnston thought that his orders were vague and his authority ill-defined—he felt he was a shadow commander, serving as a stand-in for the President. His assignment to this large domain was doubtless based on a plan which suggested itself as a result of Lee's success in northern Virginia.

Lee's army, fighting within the Department of Northern Virginia, had done extremely well. In this sector Lee had been supreme, co-ordinating the movements of all small forces. Brought together at the right time and place, Lee's combined forces had been able occasionally to meet the enemy on relatively equal terms. Lee was, then, the model exponent of efficient and effective utilization of departmental resources. Davis had stayed out of Lee's way, although Lee, the master diplomat, had never let the President feel out of touch with affairs in Virginia. What worked so well in the case of Virginia might do equally well elsewhere. Davis became acutely aware of the need for co-ordination of effort, and the west stood in the most urgent need of effective co-ordination.

Davis recognized the importance of the west, and Secretaries of War George Randolph and Seddon never let him forget it. He has been criticized for failing to do better for that area, for placing greater emphasis on Virginia, and for concentrating the best military talent in the northeast to the detriment of the west. On the surface he is guilty, but the charge is brought with the benefit of hindsight. Davis actually may be guilty of bad judgment but not of bias.

He sent to the west some commanders who failed to win. And since Lee was doing so splendidly, westerners screamed for blood. If the Army of Northern Virginia could throw back legion after legion, why was it that the Federal armies crept deeper and deeper into the west? The answer was obvious: Davis sent the dregs of military talent to fritter away the western armies. The question really revolves around a definition of terms. What constitutes a good military leader? Davis had his own ideas; the people differed with him—some of them —and events appeared to sustain the popular majority.

Who were the men—those paragons of ineptitude in the public mind—whom Davis sent west? At the head of the list would go men like John Bankhead Magruder, Benjamin Huger, and Theophilus H. Holmes. Each had failed under Lee in Virginia and had been transferred to what seemed lesser fields of mischief. These examples alone were cited as sufficient proof of the charge of eastern favoritism against Davis. Simply because these men were sent down from Lee's army and shipped to the hinterlands proved the point. The President would tolerate no mediocrity in Virginia, but did not in the least mind sending second-raters west.

Granted these men were not the best, the charge still is not proved. "Prince John" Magruder, dashing, dramatic, and nervous, had indeed seemed inadequate in the steaming swamps around Richmond. Huger, older, laced in "Old Army" regulations and techniques, had been too slow and uncertain under the strain of the Seven Days. Holmes, antiquated, domineering, and dangerously deaf, had been equally slow and ineffective in the same operations. All three were obviously not the caliber of men to be desired. But there were some extenuating circumstances. Magruder, apparently, had been ill and overtired; Huger had not been a field officer in the Old Army, but rather had been on ordnance duty for years; Holmes was perhaps the worst of the three, and his later record tends to bear out his incompetence much more forcefully than is true in the case of the other two officers.

[31]

Magruder did reasonably well in Texas, and Huger, transferred to the Ordnance Service, performed valuable duty.

Still, the west could argue that such men as these should hardly be pointed to as examples of military virtue. Davis ought to have done better by the west. He did. He sent Edmund Kirby Smith—for a time an able and competent officer—to command the Trans-Mississippi Department. Actually, though, the term "west" is at issue here. Holmes, Magruder, Huger, and Smith all were sent to the west beyond the Mississippi River. It was the west just east of the river which concerned most Confederate strategists, including Davis.

The Confederate frontiers in the middle west were for a time in doubt. Whether the South would mark its northern boundary along the Kentucky-Ohio line or along the Tennessee-Kentucky border was the question. To insure that the Confederacy got the largest possible territory in this region, in 1861 an army was assigned to the north Tennessee area under Albert Sidney Johnston. This army, which later became famous under the name of the Army of Tennessee, was second in importance only to Lee's army.

No one would say that Johnston was a bad choice as commander of this force. In fact, Albert Sidney Johnston enjoyed a marvelous (if ill-founded) popularity with the Southern people. He was a well-tried soldier who had served on frontier duty and with the army of the Republic of Texas. Everyone seemed to feel that he was the best the Confederacy had when the war started, but his sustained retreating into Mississippi dimmed public confidence in him. Davis, coming to his defense, remarked that if Johnston were no general, then the South had no generals! The people were not only upset about Johnston, but also about the generals who came after him. When he was killed at Shiloh in April, 1862, General Beauregard succeeded to command.

There was nothing really wrong with Beauregard. He was the hero of Fort Sumter and Manassas. It was common knowledge that he and the President did not get on well, and westerners were anxious to have him come from the scene of his triumph at Manassas to help them out. He was not, after his elevation to command of Johnston's army, spectacularly victorious, but he was not in the best of health. When, after a running tilt with Davis, he felt he should leave the rigors of the field to recuperate, he was followed in command by Braxton Bragg.

Bragg was a poor choice, said critics of Davis. Davis sent him to the Army of Tennessee because he was an old friend, and the President had faith in his abilities. He was no commander, even though he seems to have been a good organizer. But Bragg, to Davis' way of thinking, was the best man he had for the Tennessee assignment. The President felt

the same way about John Pemberton, which is why
he was put in command of the army charged with
defending Vicksburg. Davis believed he was doing
the best he could for the west by sending two of his
favorites there. Joseph E. Johnston's designation as
a commander over the armies of both Bragg and
Pemberton was an attempt to co-ordinate and unify
their operations.

Disappointed in the results obtained by his
friends, Davis was willing to accept the suggestions
of Secretaries Randolph and Seddon. The President was unwilling to dismiss Pemberton and
Bragg, but he became aware of the fact that their
disunited forces could not be co-ordinated from
Richmond. Johnston would have to exercise some
top-level authority in shifting troops between these
forces and in getting reinforcements to them. He
would also have to make logistical decisions for the
Department of the West and channel war supplies
where needed.

Davis, in surrendering considerable authority
over tactics, logistics, and to some degree strategy,
had come to a new idea of army organization. By
late 1862, the changing nature of war was becoming
clear to both sides. Geography affected administration. No longer could the separate army exist
entirely under the command of its own general.
Separate armies were not, somehow, separate any
longer. Each performed a function which was vital
to the over-all war effort. Consequently, individual

armies and commanders had to come under the control of some sort of unifying agency.

Ordinarily the Secretary of War would have been this agency. But distance disqualified the Secretary as a competent co-ordinator. Wise and able as were some of these men, they were not sufficiently omniscient to know all and see all that went on everywhere in the Confederacy. Since the War Office could no longer give effective direction to the war—if it ever had—some other type of supervision would have to be found.

Davis, moving cautiously, was not ready to do away with the traditional plan of army command. He was willing, however, to add to the command structure if an addition would solve the problem of unity. The idea of a large geographical command under an officer (Johnston) with equally large powers seemed to be a possible answer. What Davis attempted, in his groping toward a modern command system, was unified army command on a decentralized basis—in essence, a theater command of the sort so popular in World War II.

For various reasons Johnston failed to do what Davis and Seddon tried to give him the power and authority to do. Perhaps there was too much of West Point in Johnston and too little of the adventurer. Davis was disappointed.

Disappointed or not, the President did not abandon hope for his scheme of geographical army command. Much later in the war, after Hood had abandoned Atlanta and Sherman was plotting dire things for Georgia, Davis resurrected the idea.

To the new Military Division of the West, Davis called Beauregard, another of his pet dislikes. Beauregard seemed to be the only choice late in 1864. An officer of wide experience was needed, one used to authority. Beauregard was the only officer of full general's rank who could take a new field assignment, with the exception of Johnston, who was not a likely candidate.

Beauregard's task was even more difficult than was Johnston's before him. In his command area was Hood's Army of Tennessee, plus the forces under Richard Taylor in Alabama and Louisiana and the army under Dabney Maury, which was stubbornly clinging to Mobile. The strategical situation was poor. Sherman, with an army larger than Hood's, menaced the industrial and agricultural heart of the South. Hood had hatched a plan. He wanted to dash off on an invasion of Tennessee and threaten Sherman's communications. Although Beauregard seems to have been lukewarm about Hood's idea, he could hardly countermand it as long as the President appeared to give it his blessing. Like Johnston, he found himself with a vast area in his charge and little real authority. He tried to aid Hood by urging supplies forward, but the Tennessee plan failed.

The Army of Tennessee, plagued by logistical troubles and a vacillating general in charge, staggered into Tennessee after everyone knew what Hood had in mind. His campaign, which in Beauregard's eyes depended on surprise for success, was a matter of common conversation. He was ruinously beaten at Franklin by Schofield and at Nashville by the old "Rock of Chickamauga," and his veterans came streaming back to Georgia to "see their Uncle Joe." Again, what was wrong with Davis' command structure? Had Beauregard let him down, and if so, how? Was the fault inherent in the military situation of the South in December, 1864? Or could it be that Davis had created once again a vast shadow command presided over by a general without real power? Perhaps Davis never learned how to delegate authority.

Had he delegated authority properly his task would have been vastly easier. He could have devoted himself to achieving liaison between important branches of the war effort—the army and navy, for instance. Such liaison would have been largely a matter of diplomacy—and Davis was no diplomat. The strength of his personality became a weakness when he tried to be diplomatic and to get along with others. Accustomed by experience to getting along by himself, he was unable to promote good relations with much-needed friends. His most glaring failure at winning friends involved the Confederate Congress.

The Congress of the Confederate States of America was not an easy group to get along with, not to mention influence. But as the chief executive, Davis was dependent on Congress for the success of his policies. The story of his relations with the Congress is too well known to relate in detail, but it should be remarked that he made increasingly feeble efforts to win congressional friendship. His penchant for telling Congress what it ought to do, and for rejecting the least interference in his executive function, seriously weakened his position.

He must have been an unhappy man. Forced to deal with what must have seemed to him monstrous mediocrity in Congress, Davis saw it as his duty to preach to its members about things which needed to be done. He made his situation no easier by frequently being right.

That was part of the great misfortune of Jefferson Davis. He was often right. There is no doubt that he grew with his job, that he came more and more to a realization of what ought to be done to win the war. Was it perhaps his growing awareness of what ought to be done that made him less tolerant of a petty and captious Congress? Perhaps the President, increasingly conscious of the desperate urgency of the Confederacy's plight, took more and more upon himself. And if that is true, he should not be too severely censured for paying too much attention to details, convinced as he was of the inadequacies of others. Perhaps it was his own special curse to be the aloof man of intellect at a time calling for the more pliant man of action.

This same personality defect hamstrung Davis in his relations with some of the state governors of the Confederacy, particularly Georgia's Joseph E. Brown and North Carolina's Zebulon B. Vance. State executives always strove to promote the best interests of their states, especially in the dogma of state rights. It was part of Davis' personal nightmare that he lived to realize the dire need for a centralized government to run the war after he had so fiercely championed the rights of the individual states. But he ultimately came to this realization, which in itself reflects his growth as an administrator.

Again, that very growth worked against him. Convinced of the need for full co-operation by all the states with the Confederate government, Davis went too far in telling state governors to forget their states for the sake of the cause. To many he began to sound like a full-blown dictator, and the hostile press effectively used this against him. Not knowing how to turn the point of these attacks, Davis could only write more vitriolic and bitter letters telling his critics what they ought to do. The governors, fearful of a growing despotism, tightened control on their own state administrations to thwart Davis' centralism. To prevent strong government, they resorted to it.

Davis' peculiar personality, with its mixture of finely tuned nerves and stubborn blockheadedness, confounded his personal relationships. Tied in with

[39]

his personality quirks was the fact that he was more than a leader in his own mind—he was the conscience of his country. Right or wrong, this attitude was interpreted by the people as a holier-than-thou smugness on the part of the President. Many resented it, and some hated him for it.

Basically, of course, this sort of thing shows Davis to have been no politician at all. He could never compromise what he knew to be right. He was intellectually honest. Honesty of Davis' brand was common in the Confederate South, which, in a way, softened the blow of defeat and made the cause worthy to remember. But it made Davis less effective as the leader of a total war.

Despite his growth in office and his intellectual honesty, the President displayed certain characteristics of a little-minded man. He was able to grow only as far as his limitations would permit and there he stopped. One of his limitations was his outlook. He could recognize the basic political needs of the Confederacy, draw on his experience in Congress, and do his best to erect a working framework of government. As the national existence of the Confederate States progressed, he could see added administrative needs. But he could never quite see the need for wide delegation of military authority.

Arrested military development afflicted Davis. Though he could authorize some innovations in field command organization, the fact remains that he was too much the Secretary of War and not enough the President who was ultimately responsible for what happened to the army and navy. Quite a competent military leader in his own mind, he refused to recognize competence in others.

For the things Davis saw as essential to the winning of the war he deserves real credit. In many ways he was too big for his job. In many ways he was too small for it. Honest to a fault, austere and unbending, Davis rose above the common herd of the Confederate Congress, soldiery, and people in dedication to the cause. Too much a believer in his own military infallibility, he was too small to see how much he needed to learn. Not knowing how to command a total war at first, he generally overcommanded. But who can blame him? Lincoln did the same things during the first two years of the war, and learned only because of defeat. Davis had early successes to lead him, and successes were not, in this case, the best teachers.

Fundamentally Davis was out of place in the Confederacy. The South was in a state of revolution, as the American colonies had been less than a century earlier. Davis was called to lead this new revolution, but he was a conservative, and conservatives are not daring enough to be good revolutionaries. Could it be, then, that in this particular sense Davis was an example of a dilemma which constantly plagued and hampered the South?

Do not underrate Davis: he was a man. Surrounded by mounting frustration, unable to

fraternize with common people, and increasingly
uncertain of the South's chances of winning, he
went on to the extremely bitter end. He was occasionally too heavy handed in his leadership (which
probably stimulated the trend to state rights), and
was absolutely ineffective at getting along with
those he should have cultivated, but he never
stopped trying.

He is an appealing figure in some ways, almost
alone in the large White House on the Richmond
hill, with more and more enemies and proportionately fewer friends, and with the boundaries of his
country shrinking around him. In the midst of hostility and derision, he was yet the President. He
looked it, always. Tall, ascetic, and hard of eye, he
went on doing all he could in his awkward way to
direct the armies in retreat. In the end, of course,
his future died with his country. Label him wrong
in many things; say he was a paradox; call him
guilty of frequent misplaced confidences and
missed opportunities; say that in the final analysis
he was too enmeshed in tradition to be a successful
leader of the Confederate war effort—but credit
him with nerve.

Jefferson Davis was much like his country.

Perhaps the characteristic of Davis' which may
account most for his limited success as a military
leader was his inability to delegate authority. Nothing more clearly illustrates this inability than the
trouble he had with the various Confederates who

were Secretary of War. Some of these six men were able, conscientious, and sound, but they seem to have been misfits. Others were pliable, easygoing, and unwilling to make decisions—and this last quality was a requisite if they were to get along with the President. A rubber stamp, deferential in all matters to Davis' superior military judgment, would do well in his job. For a Secretary of War, independence was a political hope, not a human asset. One, at least, of these men was incompetent. He irked even Davis.

The quest for "yes men" indicated an interesting contradiction in Davis himself. As Pierce's Secretary of War, he had been anything but a figurehead. He had been progressive, urging many military innovations. Yet these very qualities he found intolerable in his own subordinates. It seems that the suspicion never completely left him that none but himself could be imaginative, progressive, or able enough to run the War Department.

Certainly his first choice for Secretary of War seems to bear out this idea. Leroy Pope Walker of Alabama should not have been appointed. Shortly after he assumed the office he conceded his own failure and so did the President. He was buried in the mass of details arising during the organization of the army and was not able to cope with them all. He had no real military training, and routine administrative ability was not enough to draw upon in the early months of mobilization. Unfortunately, the first Secretary of War was bound to have some effect on molding the character of the office. In Walker's case, this fact represented all but disaster. Certainly it must have been little comfort for Walker to realize that his appointment was wholly political—a fact most indicative of Davis' feelings about the War Office.

Davis was not deluded by the fancy of a short war. Realizing the cold probability of a lengthy struggle, he ought to have used ability as the sole criterion for the appointment of the civilian head of the army. Instead, political expediency was the primary consideration. The President, faced with constructing public support for his administration, as well as with creating military organizations, had to bestow cabinet rank on influential men from as wide an area as possible.

Walker numbered among the secessionists in the Alabama Democratic ranks. He had served as chairman of the Alabama delegation to the Charleston Democratic Convention, was well liked in his state, and would have made a bad enemy. As it was, he made a bad Secretary of War.

Serving in that post from February 21 to September 16, 1861, Walker achieved something of a reputation for disorganization. Be it said in his defense that the problems facing him were enough to baffle almost anyone. Relations with state governors and decisions on lines of defense and on the proper assignment of men and materiel in an attempt to meet the huge demand, in addition to such lesser problems as basic military policy, would have taxed the wisdom and ingenuity of most men. Walker failed to make a real co-ordinative effort. Perhaps more experience—one hesitates to say common sense—would have helped him. At any rate the confusion in the War Department, for which he appeared responsible, at length brought the wrath of Congress down on him, and he agreed that he should resign.

His replacement was Judah P. Benjamin, a human dynamo who had been Confederate Attorney General. Benjamin was a brilliant lawyer, with the background and experience of a successful planter. He represented the realist in Davis' cabinet—a fact not always conducive to furthering his popularity in the Confederacy. He came to the cabinet in the first stage of governmental organization and soon was a favorite of the President. As Attorney General he had not been busy and was, therefore, able to cultivate, cajole, and advise Davis. The relationship did not go unenvied in capital circles, giving rise to anti-Semitic gossip about Benjamin.

No one could doubt his personal ability. His brilliant mind, with its hunger for work, made a comparison with Walker invidious indeed to the first War Secretary. Benjamin came to the new post unaware of the chaotic legacy bequeathed him by his predecessor. He tackled the problems old and new with customary vigor and soon had some semblance of system in the department.

But he, too, was without military training or experience. His greatest qualification was a sustained ability to get along with Davis, which may, perhaps, explain why he had trouble getting along with so many others. He maintained his friendship with Davis largely by deferring to Davis' obviously superior knowledge of martial affairs. As far as office management was concerned Benjamin was effective, but his poor background and curious talent for antagonizing his subordinates proved large handicaps. He was often forced to rely on the advice of others, and his advisors were not always the best available.

In at least one famous instance Benjamin's lack of military experience led him to make a serious blunder—a blunder which could have had decisive consequences. He made the mistake of listening to some reports from disgruntled officers who had served in the western Virginia operations under Stonewall Jackson in January, 1862. Not bothering to ask for Jackson's report of the same campaign or to ask his views, Benjamin ordered the redistribution of some of Jackson's forces. Considering the action an indication of a lack of confidence in his generalship, Jackson sent in his resignation from the army. Only the wise counsel of General Joseph E. Johnston, plus the urging of the governor of

Virginia and other friends, saved Jackson to the Confederacy. Benjamin had almost lost him.

Benjamin was not wholly to blame; he was partly a victim of Davis and of circumstances. The tendency of everybody to do things about the war in a highly personal manner infected him. Then, too, he was a man to get things done. If some people got hurt in the process of cutting red tape, that was small price to pay for efficiency. To some extent this directness was one of Benjamin's virtues. But in the case of Jackson he carried it too far. The lesson was hammered home that the Secretary of War could not personally command field operations, and, significantly, nothing of the kind happened again.

The Jackson affair was not the thing that ruined Benjamin. Something far less important to future military affairs finally got him. Not many people could see the fundamental issue of command at stake in Jackson's case, but the loss of Roanoke Island was something all could resent. The loss was not Benjamin's fault, but the Confederate Congress investigated the matter, concluded that the Secretary of War was to blame, and sought to censure him. There were a lot of reasons for the attitude of Congress. The people in general seemed to distrust Benjamin and felt a sort of nameless fear of his un-Christian influence on the President. He was too suave, too cool, too competent to be real. He had to go, and he did. He went up to the office of Secretary of State. The President made the appointment to fill a vacancy, but it was really an insult to Congress, which was about to report adversely on Benjamin's conduct of the War Office. The insult was understood by all, and Congress never forgot it. But, more important, the hue and cry was not confined to Congressional halls.

Benjamin's departure from the War Department in the middle of March, 1862, marked the end of a fairly coherent administration. He made blunders, but he also achieved stability in the conduct of office business. Moreover, some decisions had been reached by the secretary—something new, certainly. Benjamin did not, however, leave behind him a firm tradition of leadership. He was unable to perform that function with competence, and he avoided it as much as Davis would permit, which means that he avoided it almost entirely. The President made the important decisions.

The Walker and Benjamin eras fixed in the mind of the Confederate people, in and out of Richmond, the idea that untrained civilians were not the ones to serve as Secretary of War. What was needed was someone who knew the purpose of the office and could bring experience and understanding to his job. Essentially, another Davis was required. Benjamin was not successful as Secretary of War. His successor did much better, but met with equal opposition.

The day of the thoroughly civilian secretary had, for the time, passed. The new incumbent could boast of varied military experience, both on land and water. At the age of thirteen George Wythe Randolph had gone to sea as a midshipman in the United States Navy. He remained with the navy for six years, finally resigning to study law. Moderately successful in practice, Randolph was not flashy and not too well known. He was, however, a grandson of Jefferson, a family connection which classed him among the gentry without further pedigree.

Randolph became a secessionist as the years passed, and it was no surprise when he was elected to the Virginia State Convention and voted to take the Old Dominion out of the Union. His past connection with military matters may have been a factor in securing his assignment to the military committee established by the convention to consider questions of state defense. When Virginia forces took the field, Randolph went along.

He organized a fashionable unit in the capital, the Richmond Howitzers, and soon became General Magruder's Chief of Artillery. After the action at Big Bethel, Virginia, in June, 1861, Randolph was mentioned in dispatches for "skill and gallantry." First a colonelcy and then promotion to a brigadier generalship came to him. And on March 22, 1862, he was named Secretary of War. For eight months he fought with the job, with the President, with discordant elements in Congress, and with dissatisfied field commanders.

Some said that Randolph was a rubber stamp to Davis and that his tenure of office was almost wholly negative. Such a judgment sells him short, but the charge that he was a rubber stamp is hard to refute. Without certain qualities of amiability and co-operativeness he could not have lasted eight months in the office; yet he was not slavish to the President. Among his virtues were a stubborn belief in his own ideas and a determination to formulate policies which he regarded as necessary for the successful prosecution of the war.

History has neglected Randolph. He was not long in the War Department and he was not as colorful as his predecessor or as influential as his successor. Yet he was a good secretary, and as the years passed, his ability became clearer to some of his contemporaries. And this ability, particularly when compared with that of others, was considerable. Not unnaturally, it went largely unacknowledged while he was in office. Here and there a favorable comment could be heard, but these were few and far between. And yet, the favorable comments came from men peculiarly well qualified to speak—men whose opinion Randolph undoubtedly valued far above those of his carping and malicious enemies. Time and fate served him well. The good days of the Confederate cause—at least in the eastern theater—came while he was managing the War Office. The Yankees were cleared from the Shenandoah Valley by the brilliant strategy of Stonewall

Jackson and the Confederate capital was freed from the threat of McClellan's siege. Lee took the offensive against Pope and inflicted a severe defeat on the Union Army of the Potomac at Second Manassas. At Sharpsburg, Maryland, the Confederate campaign across the Potomac came to grief, but this did not really dim the hopes raised by the previous stellar successes. The only dark spot was in the west, in the area along the Mississippi.

Randolph's concern for the west placed him far above his contemporaries in the Confederate hierarchy. Almost alone, he saw the necessity of bolstering the sagging Southern fortunes in the west. Here, he believed, the final decision of win or lose would be made. Time proved him prophetic. His voice, urging the case for the protection of Tennessee, Mississippi, and the vast trans-Mississippi area, was raised amid the bellows about the war's being won in Virginia. But, small as this voice was, its very insistence gained it the audience of the President. This fact alone—that Randolph got the serious attention of Davis focused on the western theater—made him a successful Secretary of War.

The plan he had was simple. Randolph visualized the whole war on a larger canvas than most Southern military thinkers. He saw the crippling effect of bigness as a factor in strategy and realized that geography was dividing the Confederacy and making it increasingly difficult to direct the war effort from Richmond. He proposed a radical scheme of decentralization, yet did not get credit for the result. Technically, it could be said that he shared the idea with his successor, but he has received almost no credit for any part in the plan to co-ordinate the operations of the armies under General Holmes in the Trans-Mississippi Department and General Bragg, east of the river. He felt that both armies should be placed under a single co-ordinating commander, and the man he wanted for the job was General Joseph E. Johnston. The united command of the two armies, plus the responsibility for the departments of Tennessee and Mississippi, would give Johnston adequate authority and resources to meet a Federal attack. In an area command of this type it might be possible to convert a war of position into a war of movement.

The combination of Holmes's and Bragg's armies did not occur. Davis apparently found it impossible to move Holmes's men across the Mississippi to join Bragg. Pressure from the delegations of the western states in Congress was growing increasingly insistent on defending the trans-Mississippi, and a further drain of manpower from that area would not be well received. The cancellation of this western plan served as the final straw. Shortly after the event, Randolph resigned from his post.

Two officers, at least, were sorry to see him go. Joe Johnston (who may have helped shape the western scheme) commented that Randolph's departure was "to the great injury of the Confederacy," and the South's able Chief of Ordnance, Colonel Josiah Gorgas, was saddened at the loss of a good man. Their opinion was based on solid grounds. Randolph had done well.

His short term as secretary produced a new spirit in the War Department. The principle of military concentration, which everyone talked about, was part and parcel of Randolph's policy. The trouble was, of course, that Randolph could have no policy. Davis allowed him comparatively small latitude of action and rebuked him in stinging language because he ordered Holmes east of the Mississippi without requesting the concurrence of the President. Randolph resigned, complaining of restricted usefulness, and his resignation was frigidly accepted.

In a way, the achievements of Randolph's administration were frustrating and negative. He was right in his concern for the west and successful in directing Davis' particular attention to that area. He was right in championing the doctrine of concentration. Confederate manpower resources were inadequate for a war of position—maneuverability was essential. Here, too, he was both successful and unsuccessful. The principle of a large unified command was finally accepted by the President, but Randolph was not around to see it put into effect. His concept of the duties of the Secretary of War was also correct: he sought to relieve the President of tedious, routine army administration. He sought, too, to think strategically and to implement his ideas. This was his great error. It was not his province to think. He could perform certain daily functions and exercise a degree of discretion in minor matters, but he was not to use his peculiar familiarity with the military situation to deprive Davis of any part of his command function.

With the quelling of the Randolph rebellion, it was probable that Davis had firmly determined the natural limits of the authority to be exercised by any future secretary. The elimination of Randolph on November 15, 1862, may have been one of the events which convinced Confederate historian Edward A. Pollard that the cabinet officers under Davis were all "cyphers."

There was an ad interim secretary who served for about a week—General G. W. Smith—and then came James A. Seddon, the most well-known Secretary of War.

The pendulum had swung once again and the era of the generals had passed: Seddon was a thorough civilian. He was also thoroughly competent—a point possibly missed by Davis when the appointment was made. His competence should have been anticipated, however, because of his extensive experience in the United States House of Representatives. Seddon, though, was of the proper background. He was a planter of good family, a follower of John C. Calhoun, and a secessionist. All of these assets offset the possible drawback of his having been elected to the first Confederate Congress. Fortunately, he did not act like a congressman, at least not like one opposed to the administration.

His willingness to work and his obvious devotion, plus his clearly displayed understanding of the need for reporting to his superior, made him appear quite satisfactory. He was appointed on November 19, 1862, and served until February of 1865, when his resignation came as a result of an altercation with the Virginia Congressional delegation, not because of trouble with the President.

One of Seddon's greatest accomplishments was his continuing friendship with Davis. The men were unlike in many ways. Seddon was widely read and was a good conversationalist, though he tended to be a bit plodding. Davis, burning with a nervous energy, was anything but plodding. Both, however, shared a defect: neither had a marked sense of humor. Revolutionaries without humor can become extremely serious, and both Seddon and Davis came to reflect a sense of history to a depressing degree.

Seddon, however, was never overburdened with the vision of fate. He worked hard, and as time passed was able to exert more and more influence on the President. This was the way he got things done. Influence instead of advice was apparently the key to Davis' strange personality, and he came to rely heavily on Seddon. When Seddon espoused Randolph's plan for a large department in the west, Davis could see merit in the scheme. When Seddon suggested that Joseph E. Johnston—whom Davis loathed—should get the command of the new department and be given virtually unlimited power to make policy and conduct operations, Davis swallowed gall but approved the appointment.

Like Randolph, Seddon saw the war in large terms. In his views on the proper conduct of the war, he fulfilled an ideal for a War Secretary: he was a civilian who had no capacity for tactics but knew what the larger objectives were. He made unremitting efforts to reinforce the major armies in the field—at the expense of lesser forces, if need be —hoping for solid results. Not only did he believe in concentration, but he continually urged the offensive. Actually, Seddon was more the aggressor than Davis, for he would have had the Confederate armies always in the enemy's country. Much Confederate soil was worth sacrificing if the war could be carried to the Yankees.

During the years Seddon served, the declining military fortune of the South restricted his chances to devise grand strategy, and he became increasingly a businessman—engaged in blockade-running intrigue, fighting supply problems, and trying to find men for the ranks. But the Department of the West serves as a good index of the sort of strategist

Seddon could have been, given a little more latitude.

Confederate military policy had for too long seemed devoted to the principle of diffusion of energy and piecemeal operations. Seddon was addicted to the idea of co-ordination of effort, a facet of his greater interest in concentration. Co-operation or concentration—whatever the name—he felt was essential to a successful offensive. The western theater of war, far removed from Richmond, could not be controlled by the War Department. If anything fruitful were to come from campaigns there, it would come only as the result of decentralization of authority. As finally arranged, Johnston's command was highly centralized as far as his own power was concerned. He was to be the sole maker of military plans in the Department of the West, which embraced Tennessee, Mississippi, and parts of North Carolina, Alabama, and Georgia.

Under Johnston's control were to be the major forces of General John C. Pemberton and General Braxton Bragg, separated from each other by a large distance, Bragg operating in Tennessee and Pemberton in middle Mississippi. Seddon's devout hope was that Johnston, by using his discretion in combining the forces in his department, could meet the Yankees on a superior, or at least equal, footing. The only responsibility Johnston had to the President or the War Department was to report his doings and request what he needed. Unfortunately, the nature of this new command—so out of keeping with old military usage—was not thoroughly understood by Johnston.

Long an ardent believer in combining the military units of the Confederacy for joint blows at the enemy, Johnston should have been the ideal choice for group command in the west. He was admirably suited to the job in all but one sense: he could not bring himself to realize the full extent of the authority entrusted to him. Corroded by long and bitter controversy and convinced that the President did not intend him to use the powers apparently granted, Johnston could not seize the opportunity offered. He brooded for months over the proper exercise of his command, bemoaning the fact that he had so much authority that in reality he had none.

Repeated assurances to the contrary by the Secretary of War never quite persuaded the general, and he could not bring himself to exercise personal control of either or both the major armies under his charge. So the chance was wasted. Bragg and Pemberton went their own separate ways, Vicksburg fell, and Johnston retreated from Jackson, Mississippi, with a small, rag-tag force. His huge department slipped away from him and the President was confirmed in his judgment of the general. There were some extenuating circumstances which Johnston could cite in his defense. His authority was never clearly defined, and he could hardly have been expected to depose army commanders hand-picked by the President, even though he might feel they were hopelessly incompetent. These are reasons for his failure to rise to the challenge, they are not excuses.

Johnston at length reverted to the status of army commander, and Seddon's great scheme of a western military empire died for lack of imagination. He has received credit for the western plan, and as it was tried, he deserves the honor. But a far harder job had already been done by Randolph, for Seddon found the President already receptive to the defense of the west. Seddon felt that Davis was the hardest man to get along with he had ever known, and it might have proved extremely difficult to sell the idea without Randolph's preliminary softening-up.

The western plans of Randolph and Seddon were essentially dissimilar. Possibly Randolph's was bolder, but, considering Davis' personality, less realistic than Seddon's. Randolph proposed to use some of the manpower resources of the Trans-Mississippi Department, combining them with Bragg's army, to defeat enemy plans in Kentucky and Tennessee. This idea clearly shows that Randolph grasped a basic failure of the Confederacy up to late 1862—the failure to utilize adequately trans-Mississippi resources in the war effort. He was trying to correct this considerable omission, but politics and want of tact on Randolph's part turned the President against the scheme despite its obvious merits.

Seddon's idea simply substituted reality for fancy and modified Randolph's strategy. He urged better use of the armies already east of the Mississippi. The principles involved were the same: decentralization, co-ordination, and concentration. Seddon proposed no less a detraction from Davis' direction of western military operations, and yet Davis could accept the proposal from him.

By his consistent championing of the cause of western military autonomy, Seddon displayed a solid grasp of a fundamental command ingredient. He felt that control of the campaigns in the west would have to come from someone close enough to the theater to understand what was happening. A campaign in Tennessee, for instance, would possibly require co-operation of supply agencies as far away as Georgia and Alabama, as well as reinforcements from equally great distances. The availability of men, transportation, and supplies needed to sustain a western campaign could not possibly be known in Richmond with complete accuracy, despite the increasing use of the telegraph. Only an over-all commander, wise in the needs of war, could cope with the size and scope of operations developing in the Mississippi Basin.

Seddon saw the uselessness of having field commanders whom the War Department did not trust. If generals were not used to the limits of their potential, then there should be no generals. Delegation of command authority was something Seddon understood from the beginning. He was always careful about not delegating too much, and thus losing all power of co-ordination over field operations.

Seddon possessed ability of a high order. He also possessed tact to a remarkable degree. There was, possibly, something noble about him. Recognizing as he did the necessity for bolder, wider-visioned administration, he sought to cajole an egocentric President into parting with constitutional prerogative. He was not completely successful in his efforts to broaden the effectiveness of Confederate high command, but he never gave up trying. He sacrificed himself to the role of apparent door-mat as a means of achieving influence.

His greatest achievement may have been the fostering of a command concept in the President's mind which has generally escaped notice. The changing nature of war was a fact slowly realized by the trained professional soldier, but Seddon, unhampered by older military doctrine and tradition, saw the need for modern methods to fight a modern war.

War in the 1860's had become total. All elements of the population were affected; all had some part in the whole effort. Seddon attempted to utilize the potential strength of the nation. He was never able, nor was anyone else for that matter, to overcome the evils of the state rights dogma, so he could never count on complete unity of feeling in the South. He advocated unpleasant measures like impressment, restrictions on foreign and domestic commerce, and stiffer conscription when it was impolitic to do so. He did these things because he felt them essential to bring forth a maximum war effort with only the partial support of the country. Everything concerned him: transportation, price schedules, labor problems, manpower, money, civilian morale—everything. Part of the frustration of his service was his own realization of the totality of war while his countrymen talked of international law, chivalry, and noncombatants.

If Seddon is judged by the criterion of fame laid down by Albert Sidney Johnston—success—then he was a failure. If, however, he is judged on the basis of breadth of vision, devotion to irksome duty, and almost Job-like patience, then he was not a failure. With another President, one who would have given him greater fields of endeavor, Seddon might well have been a great Secretary of War.

In 1865, with the Confederate States deflating like a cast-off bagpipe, the ire of the people had to be directed somewhere. The Virginia delegation in Congress thought that the blame for the critical condition of the South could be laid at the door of the cabinet. They called for its complete reorganization, and Seddon, feeling this sentiment to be an expression of their lack of confidence, resigned.

Perhaps it was just as well that he returned to private life, for he was thus spared the necessity of dutifully standing by during the final disintegration.

Again a swing of the pendulum: the last Secretary of War was a general. John C. Breckinridge, a man who a few years before had been high in the councils of the Democratic party, was appointed to the War Department on February 4, 1865. He was called from a moderately successful career as a field commander to preside over the obsequies of the Confederacy. Perhaps a military man could breathe new life into a dying organism; yet it was a little late for new hope. But hope in the South somehow never died.

The assortment of secretaries in the War Department was not duplicated in other areas of Davis' cabinet, although changes were made now and then. Two members of the cabinet clung to their posts throughout the war—Postmaster General John H. Reagan of Texas and Navy Secretary Stephen R. Mallory of Florida.

Fortunately for Mallory, the President liked him. Mallory's counsel was sought on matters far removed from naval affairs, and no criticism of his administration of the Navy Department could induce Davis to remove him. In this position, Mallory's task was to do for the navy what the various secretaries of the War Department were attempting to do for the army—organize and administer what naval forces the Confederacy could put on the oceans or on the rivers.

Mallory seemed well qualified for his post. He had had some connection with ships during various periods of his life, was interested in naval matters, and could point to his service as chairman of the Naval Affairs Committee of the United States Senate as an important asset. Political expediency undoubtedly figured in his appointment, since a cabinet post should be assigned to Florida. Friendship was another factor, for he and Davis were longstanding friends. He was not an office seeker, but was not disposed to shirk an office when it was thrust upon him.

A recent biographer, Joseph T. Durkin, in *Stephen R. Mallory: Confederate Navy Chief,* ventures that Mallory was not necessarily a genius, but was, in 1861, "a capable and earnest small-town official trying with no small degree of confidence to fill a post that a statesman of unique and pre-eminent qualities, with a thorough grasp of naval history and unusual administrative gifts, would have found a fair field for his powers." No one would deny that his post was challenging, for there were myriad challenges and mountainous problems appearing every day.

Few people in the new Confederacy faced a quandary equal to that confronting the Secretary of the Navy when the government was formed. Like the Chief of Ordnance, Mallory's problems

Rise and Fall of the Confederate Government

CONFEDERATE CABINET MEMBERS

were complicated by the scarcity of manufacturing establishments in the South. Without adequate shipbuilding facilities, the Navy Department would have to resort to other means of obtaining ships. Money, too, was scarce, and Congress was usually stingy in its naval appropriations. Money was essential, of course, to all phases of naval operations, and the Navy Department existed throughout the war as a sort of poor relation to the War Department.

Given the inadequate resources of the Confederacy, Mallory, like many of the other Southern administrators, was compelled to contract for shipbuilding and for naval supplies. The idea of contracting with a private firm for the building of vessels had considerable appeal. For one thing it would relieve the Navy Department of much detail and would put all the pressure on the contractor. In addition, labor problems would be the contractor's to solve. Many contractors, however, found the scarcity of currency, manpower, and materiel more than they could combat. Mallory did not put all of his hopes in domestic manufacturing.

To Europe and England were dispatched naval agents—perhaps the most famous being James D. Bulloch—to purchase and to contract for the building of warships. This idea was extremely good. Particularly successful were the efforts, not always involving the navy, to build blockade-runners in Europe and England. Several good cruisers came from the foreign purchasing venture, but never enough to allow the Confederate Navy to carry out all of its missions.

Standing at the top of the list of missions for the navy was defense of the coastal waters. The army was responsible for the defense of the coast itself, but protection of more than three thousand miles of coastline, of all the remote little roadsteads, inlets, bays, and inland rivers would fall to the navy. Only at the larger ports, partially defended by fortifications, could the navy count on the help of land-based artillery and army support. For the rest of the way, the navy was on its own. The Marine Corps, pitifully small, was of little use. Mallory saw clearly enough that the Confederacy needed light steam gunboats, some of large size with heavier ordnance, and a few monster ironclads.

Mallory's reliability seems to have been one of the reasons why Davis left him more latitude of activity than the Secretary of War. Moreover, the President possibly realized that he knew far less of naval matters and should stay out of the way. The fact remains that Mallory was able to exercise much more direct control over the navy than the numerous secretaries of the War Department ever exerted over the army. For this reason, he was much more the real commander of the navy. He originated policy and strategy and co-ordinated the activities of his subordinates, with whom he usually got along well. The idea of commerce raiders and the decision to use ironclad gunboats were his, and the President acquiesced.

It is certain that part of the success which Mallory achieved was due to the nonintervention of Davis in Navy Department management. This is not to say that Davis was uninterested in what Mallory was doing. On the contrary, he seems to have offered him steady encouragement. But beyond encouragement and sympathy he does not appear to have gone. Consequently, Mallory could count on continuity of policy, as could all other naval personnel. The sustained amiability of relations between the President and the Secretary of the Navy indicated a long tenure of office, which in turn meant unwavering and solid administration. Sometimes, however, navy policy was poorly received by the public.

The navy was a convenient scapegoat. Nobody really expected much from it and as a result it was easy to ridicule. Mallory and his subordinates were not infallible—they made mistakes, but fewer by volume than many other Confederates. Some could argue, of course, that the restricted scope of naval operations restricted the possibility of error. Such an attitude was hardly just to the navy. Working with limited resources, less money, and few ships, Mallory's department did well.

The commerce-raiding policy may be considered a partial success. Federal shipping was virtually driven from the seas and forced to cower under neu-

[67]

tral banners. A clear view of the impossibility of the Confederate Navy's slugging it out ship for ship with the Yankees produced the war cruiser, a vessel best exemplified by the *Sumter,* the *Alabama,* the *Florida,* and the *Shenandoah.* Versatile, swift, and tough, the cruisers of Secretary Mallory wrote a new page in the history of naval warfare. They performed a function as hard-hitting warcraft and merchant destroyers, and dry statistics would offer impressive evidence of the success of their careers. Suffice it to say that they became dread specters to many a Yankee trader, but they failed to draw off a great number of Federal ships from blockade duty.

With the passage of time and consequent growth of experience, better use was made of cruisers. Random destruction was replaced by carefully planned economic warfare. Machine lubrication was an increasingly important factor in the Union war effort, and whale oil consequently took on great significance. The Confederate raiders were finally used against whaling fleets, and if this had been done earlier it is possible that much Union machinery would have run dry.

Economic warfare was vital in the Civil War. Few people, however, understood it or conceived it as an arm of a national conflict which could be applied directly. Mallory was one of its few practitioners, and it was one of his more important activities.

Mallory was responsible for yet another important innovation. Ironclad warships were not unknown before 1861, despite considerable superstition to the contrary. France had the huge *Gloire* (which Mallory tried unsuccessfully to buy), and there were others. The Secretary of the Navy's decision to build and use ironclads was daring. Common sense supported the scheme. The Union Navy consisted of numerous imposing ships of the line, bristling guns from heavy-timbered hulls. And in timber, possibly, lay their doom. Ironclads could get close enough to demolish wooden ships either by shelling or ramming. Naval ordnance in the early 1860's had not progressed to the stage of the armor-piercing shell, so a few ironclads could do the work of many old-style ships. In ironclads, then, the Confederate Navy would specialize and spend most of its limited resources in a desperate gamble with progress. It almost paid off.

The epic fight between the Confederate ironclad *Virginia* (*Merrimac*) and the Federal ironclad *Monitor* is well known. It marked an end and a beginning. It spelled *finis* to Mallory's dream of a fleet of unchallenged iron monsters wrecking Northern ports and ruining the Union Navy, but it opened a new era in United States naval history. Lincoln's Secretary of the Navy, Gideon Welles, plus the responsible Federal naval officers, were slower to realize the value of boiler plate attached to ship hulls than were the Confederates. Their sloth might have lost the naval war to a nation with

[69]

no navy to speak of and no standing among the powers of the earth.

Ironclads were used by the Confederacy throughout the remainder of the war, but their power was broken by bigger, better, and faster ones coming from the Northern shipyards.

The final failure of the Confederate Navy was not Mallory's fault. He deserves to be remembered for having revolutionized war on the high seas and for his breadth of view.

In one instance only he was narrow. His imagination never seems to have been stirred by the possibilities of blockade-running on a large scale. Only infrequently did he permit navy personnel to participate in running the blockade, even on government ships. Never did he like to have navy vessels involved in this business, and it is doubtful if any navy ship ever officially ran the blockade carrying freight.

Had Mallory made a determined bid to have the navy take over and supervise all Southern shipping, Confederate foreign-purchasing ventures might have been far more fruitful. He should have permitted more navy officers to engage in blockade-running unofficially. This he could have arranged without embarrassing anyone—not even the President. Broad as was the vision of this able secretary, it was not broad enough to make better use of one of the Confederacy's few chances for success.

Mallory did not always do well in other areas.

Sometimes relations between the Navy Department and the War Department grew strained. The growing scarcity of supplies forced the departments into competition on the open market, and this led to additional rivalry. Secretary Randolph seems to have gotten along better with Mallory than any of the other men who were Secretary of War. While Seddon served in the War Office, the navy enjoyed continuing fair relations with the army, but Randolph was missed by Mallory. Randolph was cooperative; Mallory was too, to some extent, but he grew touchy. Manpower problems drove both the army and navy into a race for skilled mechanics, and neither was any too willing to part with good men for the benefit of the other. This sort of friction intensified as time passed.

Mallory should not be censured too severely for his "navy first" attitude. Even had he been more generous with the resources of his department, he might not have met with similar generosity on the part of the army, and the navy would have lost valuable property to no advantage. Perhaps, after all, it was not wholly the responsibility of each secretary to allocate critical goods to other departments—particularly when his own department needed such goods so badly. Rationing of resources should have been a command function of a higher authority.

The problem was one of unification of effort. The secretaries of the two services should have gotten together for purposes of working out ways and means of helping each other, but they never really did. On the surface, at least, there seemed little need for mutual assistance.

The general outline of the war made it clear that the army was the most important cog in the Confederate military machine. The navy ran an extremely lame second. This attitude was reflected in cabinet sessions, Congressional appropriations, and in popular thinking. The army did the hard work and the navy did what little it could with so few resources. About all that could be expected of Mallory's outclassed tubs was a spectacular raid or two, or possibly a great joust such as that between the *Virginia* and the *Monitor* or the *Alabama* and the *Kearsarge*. In essence the navy was almost a fiction which Southern pride kept up. Or so thought most of the army, at any rate.

Actually this was a misconception of the proper function of the navy. Mallory and some of his able subordinates, it will be remembered, were aware of the useful duties which the navy could perform. On a few occasions the navy was able to assist the army in a combined military operation, and it was not entirely the fault of the sailors that these ventures (such as the attack on Baton Rouge in 1862) misfired. Combined operations on a large scale were fairly new tactics, and the fact that the Confederacy tried this sort of thing at all speaks well for some of the high command.

The command failed in not carrying combined efforts further. The navy had a good many trained officers who could have been of great use to the army in the later stages of the war. The reverse was true, to some extent, for the army could have helped the navy, particularly by sending to the sister service needed skilled laborers.

Some naval artillerists did assist in manning land batteries, but usually not without considerable squabbling about who was in charge of the installations—witness the case of Drury's Bluff in the James River defenses. Moreover, some navy ordnance supplies got into the needy hands of the Army Ordnance Bureau, but only after long and harrowing delay and bickering.

The army brought some of the navy's lack of co-operation on itself. By refusing to permit the transfer of vitally needed skilled laborers to the navy's Bureau of Ordnance and Hydrography, the Secretary of War incurred the hostility of Mallory. But the President was somewhat to blame. Had he taken steps to insure instant mutual assistance on the part of his service secretaries, the picture might have been changed. When he was appealed to for arbitration of a conflict between the army and navy, Davis doubtless tried to be fair, but the army usually won out. This is not hard to understand. After all, the army's troubles were obvious and fairly close at hand. The army had had substantial successes, and the navy had had unfortunate disap-

[73]

pointments. The war could be won on land; the army had a chance, while the navy could only sting the extremities of the United States fleet. So it was that the President failed to provide an executive liaison between the land and water branches of the military establishment which would have increased the effectiveness of both.

Left alone, Mallory got the most from himself. Beginning his secretaryship with moderate experience and only slightly-above-average talent, the navy chief grew with his responsibilities. Not discounting his errors and mistakes in judgment, the conclusion is inescapable that his administration of the Navy Department is one of the bright pages in the history of the executive branch of the Confederate government.

The Confederate States of America was founded on republican principles, hence the executive's responsibilities and powers were restricted and divided. Since the judicial branch of the government was never in full operation, only the executive and legislative branches meant anything. The Confederate Congress did much during the war, and its role was far more significant than is generally realized. Acting in the image of its Yankee counterpart, Congress had control of appropriations, and, despite the scarcity of real money in the South, it provided for continuing the war with makeshift finances. Next in importance to its financial role came Congress' function as a directing agency of the war effort.

While it is true that the Confederate Congress created no Joint Committee on the Conduct of the War to interfere with all military matters, several investigative committees were set up to examine the effectiveness of war planning. This was a legitimate function of Congress, and it was unfortunate only that a better job of intelligent investigating was not done.

Congress, like all such bodies, was human and subject to human failings. Its perversion of power was one of the worst of its failings. It had a good many members with long and distinguished legislative careers, and this, so they thought, qualified them above all others—including the President and military men—to run the war. The only thing wrong with this idea was that there were too many such experts. The resultant confusion and disagreement hurt the Confederate cause.

The most obvious duty of Congress was to serve as a reflection of the public attitude toward the war, and when the public was in error, it was the task of Congressional leaders to try to inform and direct opinion in the right direction.

The moulding of public opinion could have been the most effective job done by Congress. But it was not. Instead of maintaining close relations with the people, Congress tended to become isolated in

Richmond. Such isolation was well-nigh fatal. When the desperate urgency of events demanded a basic change in Confederate attitudes toward such things as state rights, impressment, and taxation, Congress was not close enough to its constituents to influence them.

This is not to say that no one in Congress knew what was going on. Some of the debates—often endless wrangling over minute trivia—might lead to that suspicion, but the suspicion would be largely wrong. Most members had some idea of what had to be done, but frequently differed on how to do it. They were confused by factions within their own ranks, some representing business, others representing individual generals, and still others supporting one or another cabinet member (not to mention the state interests always prevalent), and they were confused as well by poor presidential direction.

When Congress was confused and divided about the proper course of action, the President should have stepped in with real executive leadership. Because Davis had himself become isolated from Congress after 1863, and because he chose to grow even further removed from it, his leadership was lacking at crucial times. The President often bemoaned the failure of Congress to do what ought to have been done, but he was partially to blame. The only ideas he gave Congress of what he wanted were almost all contained in his official messages, and these were often phrased in brittle, uncompromising terms.

Congress has been accused of diffusing its energy, of going off in different directions and not concentrating on winning the war. The pitiful sum of the Erlanger Loan can be cited as an indication that Congress was small-minded in its financial policy and unable to spend big to win a big war. The Confederate Congress was conservative, and conservative men were thinking ahead to future generations when they failed to authorize more than a $15,000,000 loan, even though the lender would have advanced much more.

Conservatism did not, however, cloud the vision of Congressional leaders all the time. Frequently large appropriations were asked for by various military agencies, and almost always granted. It was in other ways that Congress' miserliness hurt. Feeling deeply the old dislike for big government, the Confederate Congress could not bring itself to tax as much as the emergency demanded. By backing into a financial program Congress committed a fatal error. Inflation, growing worse as the result of no real tax policy, has been cited as a primary cause of Confederate disintegration.

Essentially Congress was willing to do what seemed necessary to win the war. But the leaders of both houses were haunted by distrust of the military leadership and could never feel complete confidence in any of these officials, save their own particular pets. Without faith in the Secretary of War, and in other department heads, Congress was always cautious. And its fear of the Secretary of the Treasury was most serious.

Ridden by confusion, diseased by suspicion, and frightened by military reality, Congress did fairly well. With little help from the President, the character of Confederate legislation is surprisingly good. Congress, after much hesitation, could face up to cold facts and take some bitter medicine. The members, striving for state and individual rights, could bring themselves to legislate such unpleasant things as martial law, impressment, higher taxes (not high enough), and economic controls. True, much of this legislation was too lenient and misdirected, but that it was passed at all indicates that Congress was not totally blind to the new nature of total war.

Civilian administration of the Confederate war effort cannot be considered a success, since, after all, the Confederacy was defeated. Civilian leaders of the South, though, were not entirely to blame. They were compelled to act according to their training, and this may well have been their undoing. Trained in the tradition of small government, they could not see war as a full national effort for some time. Caught in the tradition of an agrarian economy, they could not see war as a big business.

CHAPTER THREE

Command and the Factor of Logistics

L OGISTICS was not a common word in 1861. By definition it means the moving, provisioning, and quartering of troops, and, also by definition, it is regarded as a branch of military science. Science, however, had not so far expanded into the field of war by the 1860's to require a special word for commonplace problems. The moving, quartering, and feeding, as well as arming, of troops had been a relatively simple matter in previous American wars.

Certain it was that Washington's army suffered from various deficiencies in supplies during the Revolution, and there were some notorious supply lapses in the War of 1812 as well as in the Mexican War. Nonetheless, the problem was not so large that it required big and extremely specialized agencies on a national scale.

Usually the staff departments simply purchased what the armies needed on the open market, or contracts were let to various transportation companies, supply houses, and landholders. Such details could be handled by the well-known offices of the War Department: the Quartermaster General, Commissary General, and, a bit later, the Chief of Ordnance. These officials did not maintain elaborate offices with myriad subordinates in charge of complicated details. The running of these offices was essentially personal, easily managed, and only moderately confused by red tape.

In previous wars the handling of supplies and transportation had been regarded as a staff function exclusively—a matter which certainly did not involve command decisions. Sometimes supply matters drew the attention of army commanders (witness the case of Washington), but only because of the simplicity of army organization, with commanding generals doing many things themselves which staff officers would do for them in later years. As time passed, it became the custom for army, division, brigade, and regimental commanders to have officers attached to their staffs charged with transporting, feeding, clothing, and arming the unit. The arrangement extended as far down as company level, with quartermaster, ordnance, and commissary sergeants handling these matters.

Such a refinement of the supply function should have worked in the crisis of 1861. But it did not, because this crisis was more massive than all previous ones. Time would pass, however, before the

RAILROAD TURNTABLE, ATLANTA, GEORGIA

ARMY WAGON PARK

old organization would prove itself inadequate and a whole new idea of logistics would emerge.

The Confederacy was to discover that the machine age had brought with it a new type of warfare. Improvements in transportation—particularly the development of the railroad—ushered in a new era in war. No longer were military operations completely restricted by the limitations of wagons, horses, and human feet. Now it was possible to conquer distance and use geography as a factor in strategy. Large armies could be transported large distances in comparatively short times.

The advent of the war of movement on a mass scale introduced a number of new problems. These mass armies, as they were shunted around various theaters of war, must be supplied with food, clothing, ammunition, and means of local transport. So mass war meant mass logistics. The problem of supply grew in direct ratio to size of forces in the field, and the large armies of the 1860's outgrew the yearly estimates of supply officers on both sides. As the armies expanded, the older, simpler systems of supply became antiquated. War had become so big that whole segments of the economy of the nation were caught up in it.

Logistics became, as a result, an economic system. The staggering size of the Confederate war effort required the allocation of all national resources to best advantage. No element of the country was unaffected. The mobilization of the economy for war posed a problem so basic that it embraced all echelons of command, as well as of the economy. Money, manpower, transportation, and industrial and agricultural production were all involved from the outset—though the importance of some may have been missed for a time. Before long it was clear that foreign commerce would figure as a large factor in the war effort, although how it could be exploited to best advantage was a baffling question.

Management of the nation's economy for logistical purposes was really the heart of the war effort. It could be reduced to relatively simple terms, as expressed by Jefferson Davis early in the war when he said that if troops had food, arms, and ammunition they could fight. This they could do, even without clothing and shelter, although it would behoove the supply agencies to try to avoid the possibly bizarre appearance which overemphasis on food and munitions might produce.

Reduced to essentials, then, logistics involved the feeding, clothing, shelter, medical care, and arming of the troops to the best advantage. No one had to be told that if these functions were not performed, there would be no Confederate armies—indeed, no war.

It was easy to explain the importance of logistics, and this very ease may have helped confound the problem. To many people, the matter of making ready an army for field duty was not unlike the commonplace business of readying individuals for daily activities. This attitude, as a matter of fact, has been reflected in military histories of almost all wars. The drama of battle (along with the outstanding personalities of the conflict) is what captures the attention of the historian. Almost no attention is given to the tremendous labor required of so many behind the lines before the battles could have taken place at all. Supplies are taken for granted. Matters of logistics are dull, require much drudgery to dig out, and make boresome reading. Why bother with such things? This sort of approach has largely been apparent in the histories and biographies concerning the Civil War. There simply is no comparison, from the standpoint of interest, between the battles of Jackson's campaign in the Shenandoah Valley and the problems encountered by his chief quartermaster officer during the same campaign. But a strong case may be made for asserting that the activities of Jackson's quartermaster were a key to the general's success in the Valley.

Co-ordination was the essence of logistics—co-ordination of procurement, of transportation, and of distribution. Merely buying or impressing military supplies was not enough. Nor was it enough to transport supplies from the places of purchase to the various theaters of war. Both of these activities had to be co-ordinated so that the distribution of supplies to the armies was timely and efficient. Supplies which arrived too late, or too far from the

[83]

distribution points, were no help. An overstock of supplies for an army could, on the other hand, constitute a terrific problem if a rapid movement became necessary.

Real co-ordination was slow to come. The Confederacy, like the Union, started the war with the supply services of the old United States Army. This supply organization, following the general structure of the army, was essentially simple. The Quartermaster General stood as the ranking staff officer (next to the Adjutant General), followed by the Commissary General of Subsistence, and then by the Chief of Ordnance (there was no separate Ordnance Bureau listed in the War Department, but to all intents and purposes this bureau was an entity separate from the Corps of Artillery). For a time the Chief of Ordnance doubled as the Chief of Engineers, reflecting the comparative smallness of the Engineer Corps. The Surgeon General, in charge of the Medical Corps, had a small office with few assistants and never seemed to be considered on the same level with the other service chiefs. He was a doctor, and could never aspire to a line command. In the thinking of the other staff officers, he was a cut below them.

It was not long after the initial organization of the staff departments before refinements took place. The problems raised by large masses of men coming into the ranks dictated enlargement of the staff units, larger offices, and specialized functions. The

Secretary of War permitted the setting up of the Signal Service in the War Department, albeit somewhat subordinated to the other services. In no area was the growing specialization of war more apparent than in the Ordnance Bureau. As the necessity grew for arming more and more men and for providing artillery and ammunition for the armies and for the coastal defenses of the Confederacy, so grew the need for more men in the Ordnance Bureau. This duty required a special type of personnel —men with ordnance, engineering, and scientific skills. This became more and more apparent as the services of the bureau expanded.

The peculiar situation of the Confederacy to some extent contributed to confounding the problems of the bureau. Naturally the blockade made it increasingly necessary to develop the domestic manufacturing resources of the South, but many of the functions which had to be performed by the Confederate Ordnance Bureau were duplicated by its Union counterpart. What really was breaking down the old simplicity of things was the complex nature of mass slaughter.

Mass war meant massive firepower. The Ordnance Bureau had to deliver to the various Confederate armies sufficient amounts of cartridges and shells to sustain the incredibly big battles of total war. Not only that, but the bureau also had to provide sufficient reserves for extended campaigns (witness, for example, Lee's two invasions of the

North, Bragg's Kentucky campaign, and Hood's Tennessee venture).

Since the rate of cartridge consumption by one soldier during a battle ranged anywhere from twenty-five to fifty, the problem of obtaining an adequate supply of lead became acute. This problem was duplicated in relation to all other metal resources. Iron, steel, and bronze for artillery and small arms production and copper and zinc for percussion cap manufacture were all in short supply. The Ordnance Bureau was expected to deliver these goods, but it first had to find adequate raw materials.

Location and development of mineral resources was too much of a chore for the bureau, added to its normal duties of obtaining, transporting, and distributing arms, guns, and ammunition to the field armies and forts. Consequently it became necessary to add another bureau to the War Department and take some of the burden off the shoulders of Ordnance. The Nitre and Mining Corps, charged with finding and developing all the mineral resources of the Confederacy, was formed in April, 1862. This corps, at first a part of the Ordnance Bureau, was finally made a separate bureau and grew powerful.

In 1864 the Bureau of Foreign Supplies, also originating in the Ordnance Bureau, was added to the War Department's growing list. The concern of Ordnance for foreign sources of munitions had involved that bureau so heavily in blockade-running that it required a special group of officers to handle all the business connected with running ordnance into the South through the Union fleets. As blockade-running expanded, it became impossible for the Ordnance Bureau to attend to it, and the responsibility was transferred to the new agency.

These two new bureaus will serve to indicate the sort of specialization taking place in the war. As more agencies were created to handle special areas of logistics, it became increasingly difficult to co-ordinate the efforts of all the supply services.

Traditionally, co-ordination of these efforts came from the top. The President, through the Secretary of War and the Secretary of the Navy, directed the whole business of supplying the army and navy. The Secretary of War, then, should have co-ordinated the efforts of all army supply agencies. There are several reasons why this War Department co-ordination often proved inefficient.

Frequently the civilian secretaries were not competent to perform this task. This was not always true, since some of them were able administrators who made strenuous efforts to see that duplication and overlapping of functions were kept to a minimum. Gradually, though, the secretaries left the matter of co-operation to the bureau chiefs in much the same way that the President delegated logistical authority to the secretaries. This decentralization at the top was to prove dangerous.

Delegation of authority to co-ordinate was a mistake. When the Secretary of War abdicated this function, he put too much strain on the bureau chiefs. Each of these departmental officers was too close to his own department and too involved in the fierce competition for money, labor, and materials to take a detached view of the supply problem. These men were responsible for the efficient performance of their own departments, and, keenly feeling that responsibility, could hardly be expected to sacrifice something of the efficiency of their own bureaus for the benefit of a, competing service. Because there was no single directing hand, they frequently duplicated the functions of other departments and engaged in ruinous competition for scarce materials. Considering the nature of the jobs these various bureaus were expected to perform, their apparent selfishness is understandable.

The problems of all the War Department supply agencies were similar: procurement, transportation, and distribution. Procurement, the basic function, was first a matter of money. This remained true even if the Confederate supply agencies did not purchase supplies but manufactured them on government account. Money was necessary to run the government plants, and money was increasingly hard to find.

Confederate finance is an involved story in itself, and much too long to be discussed here. The stark fact about money which most concerned supply officers was that it was scarce and grew scarcer and less valuable as the war progressed. Inflation, the result of many complicated factors, ruined the currency, which finally became all but worthless. One modern historian, the late Charles W. Ramsdell, long a student of Confederate economic problems, felt that the decline in the value of money was basic to the whole economic structure. "Depreciation and enhancing costs," he said, "called for more treasury notes which resulted in further depreciation and higher prices; and thus the vicious downward spiral, once entered upon, could not be stopped until utter ruin had resulted."

Once the public confidence in Confederate money had been undermined, the troubles of the services of supply were hopelessly multiplied. Then it became impossible to persuade Southern citizens to sell sorely needed commodities to the army. When that happened there was but one thing left to do—a thing which would cause resentment, hatred, and no little resistance on the part of the people—impress what was needed.

So, then, procurement was also a matter of market. Supplies had to be available. During the early part of the war, it will be recalled, most of the supply agencies relied on the simple plan of open market purchasing. These were the good days when the war would not last long and when economy was a theory, not an agonizing matter of daily practice. The markets of the South offered what seemed ample for the war. Food could be purchased in abundance, and there would be no scarcity of material for cotton uniforms. Of the real sinews of war —machines, metals, and men—there seemed no serious shortage at first.

But things changed. The Confederate infantry marched without shoes as leather grew scant. Hard, battle-toughened veterans sometimes looked funny —or pathetic—in ragged suits of assorted patches when new clothing became rare. Horses, in the wagon traces or pulling artillery, shrank to skeletons as forage gave out. The good days gave way to a long, deadly trial of privation and want. Somehow the armies had to be maintained in spite of attrition.

As supplies became scarce, the various bureaus increased their efforts to buy on the open market. Each of the bureaus, growing desperate to fulfill its supply goal, cast caution to the winds and upped the bidding, doing its best to outbid the other services. This sort of practice naturally resulted in making inflation worse and in cutting the throats of sister bureaus. Another evil grew out of this competition. Sometimes, when a particularly good market was found, a bureau would purchase far more than it required of some commodity ("stockpiling" is the current word) just to insure against future poverty. This left other agencies which might have needed that very commodity with no resources. Here is where a central procurement agency could have been of inestimable value to the Confederate war effort.

Competition, combined with inflation, finally ruined the open market system of procurement. Then it was that the Quartermaster General, Commissary General, Chief of Ordnance, Surgeon General, and all the other service heads resorted to a potent reserve power delegated to them by the Secretary of War—impressment. The commandeering of private property which constitutes impressment was an accepted war practice. In a sense, by resorting to it, the government was simply exercising eminent domain over all types of private supplies, and even in the Constitution-minded Confederacy this was a recognized governmental prerogative. But it was a power to be used sparingly and with extreme caution. That was the trouble— not enough caution was used. The Constitution implied the right to impress, with "just compensation," so the War Department felt no qualms in authorizing its supply bureaus to take what they needed.

There is no doubt that the War Department was too hasty in conferring the authority to take private property, but there were urgent requests, as early as 1862, for such power. Rules were prescribed by the Secretary of War which were designed to protect citizens against illegal seizure or undue hardship, but rules were not always sanctified in war zones and the arrogance of the military was hard to bear.

Complaints came in from many irate individuals. Quartermaster or commissary or some other officials had descended and taken what they wanted without observing any formalities at all—merely saying they were armed with authority from the War Department and giving a certificate of impressment to the outraged owner. These certificates, often issued spuriously, were extremely hard to translate into money—a fact which did the reputation of the government for prompt payment no good at all.

Nor did it do the government any good to have agents of some supply bureaus take private property while ample supplies were available on the open market. This sometimes happened because supply agents did not wish to be bothered with competing for these supplies, and sometimes because such agents were dishonest and impressed goods which they then sold for their own profit. Such occurrences tended to discredit the whole system of impressment.

Complaints became so general and so serious that finally Congress took up the matter, and in March, 1863, passed an act regulating impressment. This act was expected to eliminate iniquities in the system by setting up rules of fair appraisal and clear channels of payment. In time, however, it had to be amended, for ways were found to elude its provisions. Gradually it became clear to everyone that impressment, once established as a government practice, would never please everybody. There were always agents out for themselves, as well as civilian soreheads who so resented losing anything to the army that they complained about the smallest and most legitimate impressments.

Impressment worked increasing hardship as money was inflated. As a rule, property was taken at the official schedule price, which was usually far under the market value. And even then owners were often paid in the abominable certificates of indebtedness, which carried not even the dignity of a promissory note. Little wonder that hoarding was stimulated by impressment. Anything seemed justified as long as a person could keep his goods out of the tainted hands of impressment officers.

Obviously impressment should have been avoided, for it was one of the most demoralizing actions of the Confederate government. But what else could be done? With finances in a pitiful state, and constantly growing worse, it became impossible to buy supplies, even had they been available for purchase. Without money people were not going to step up and volunteer their horses, food, and cotton to the government without a bit of persuading. Since the need was great, impressment seemed imperative. Even the advantage of hindsight offers no other possibility. Impressment was a mistake, but a mistake which the crazy quilt of the Confederate economic structure forced on the government.

Efforts were made by the supply services to get along without impressment. When money was available, contracts were let to various private firms to manufacture needed goods such as uniforms, shoes, camp and garrison equipage, arms, and munitions of all kinds. But here, again, a central directing agency was lacking. Such an agency, which would have had charge of all government contracts, could have prevented several bureaus contracting for the same things and could have established priority for scarce materials.

As a result of no central authority, the contract system of procurement was caught in the same whirlpool as all other systems. Each contractor, when he ran short of labor or raw materials, would appeal to the Quartermaster General, or to whichever supply chief he was beholden for his contract. The appeal usually produced efforts to obtain the necessary items, either by purchase or impressment, and so the cycle continued. Not always, but frequently, the private contractors found the pressure of financing and working their shops too much for them. They were pressed to the wall by inflationary material and labor costs. Even periodic contract price adjustments by the government could not always save these firms. As a result, they either defaulted on the contracts or had to sell out to the government.

This business of contractors' foreclosing on their own mortgages and turning their plants over to the government presented an awkward problem. None of the supply agencies was anxious to become a manufacturer. Not only was it possibly contrary to the free enterprise concept of government, but it was certainly not efficient. Far better was the system of letting the individual contractors fight to obtain labor and materials. It was no fun at all when the supply bureaus were forced to undertake such efforts on their own.

Pressure of circumstances, though, more and more made the various bureaus small manufacturing empires in themselves. What happened to them is not hard to see. Their contractors had given up the ghost because of inflationary prices and cutthroat competition. Many of these contractors, anxious to aid the government, believed they were doing the best thing by selling out to the supply services. This was not an unnatural belief—surely these agencies would have ways and means of eliminating the problems that had beaten private industry. The government departments with their impressment and conscription powers could certainly get raw materials and labor to run the plants. The trouble was they could not.

One reason they could not lies in the nonexistence of a centralized agency charged with logistics. Here is one of the signal failures of the Confederate government. Though much legislation was passed aimed at regulating branches of the economy—so much, in fact, that one modern writer was inspired to write a monograph titled *State Socialism in the Confederate States of America*—the efforts were too haphazard to produce really effective regulation.

Had control of logistics been effectively handled by executive authority, a fatal paradox might have been avoided. An agency with sufficient power to manage the Confederate war effort could have made centralization mean something. Ordinarily, when contractors were forced by the deteriorating economic situation of the South to sell out to some government department, the increased centralization of procurement could have been an asset. But as it was, centralization of effort occurred only on a piecemeal basis. Each department could, as a result of a contractor's demise, centralize its own particular efforts, but it had no knowledge of what another department was doing unless an unusually friendly atmosphere existed between them. So instead of making for more efficient operations, the increased responsibility of each department only made things worse.

Instead of reducing duplication and competition, growing centralization of supply functions in each agency made these evils larger. The trouble was that centralization did not go far enough. While each bureau was forced to centralize, the War Department itself remained generally decentralized. Here was a dilemma which seems to have gone unrecognized.

C.S.S. *STONEWALL*

RUINS OF RICHMOND, FROM THE JAMES RIVER

Procurement posed problems other than markets, contracts, and impressment. Almost as fundamental as money to procurement was labor, which became increasingly important as more and more factories came under government control. These industries required numbers of skilled workers—men, and sometimes women—to run machines and execute skilled hand work. But this type of labor was another of the commodities which were in short supply in the South. There may have been enough artisans and mechanics available had it been possible to funnel them to the places where they were most needed. This could have been done, because the conscription laws gave the government power to enroll almost all male citizens and to detail them for duty wherever necessary. So the Bureau of Conscription could have served as a national skilled-labor agency, giving priority to those industries most fundamental to the war effort.

Things were not quite so simple. In defense of the Conscription Bureau—which needs all the defense it can get—it is only fair to say that there was some confusion over who had the final word on manpower assignment. The bureau apparently conceived its sole duty to be the gathering of men for the ranks. What happened to this human raw material, once caught up in the war machine, was somebody else's problem. This somebody else was the Secretary of War.

Allocation of critical manpower—in this case

skilled labor—to essential war industry was never efficiently done. The Secretary of War was not fully aware of the seriousness of the problem for a year at least. By the time the Quartermaster and Ordnance Bureaus convinced the War Department of their desperate need for skilled labor, much of that labor pool was already in the ranks. Once in, it usually proved difficult to get men out. Orders from the Secretary of War were necessary, and such orders almost always drew hot and angry words from army commanders, who needed every man they had. As a result, details from the ranks were kept to a minimum, and as the war went on and manpower dwindled, they all but stopped.

They should not have stopped, of course. The Chief of Ordnance argued constantly that such a policy was the worst sort of pound-foolishness. What good was an army without supplies? And there would certainly be no supplies if the staff departments were unable to keep the clothing factories, arsenals, armories, powder works, and harness shops running. No more forceful evidence in support of this contention could be offered than the Chief of Ordnance's assertion, in 1864, that the death of one Richmond armory barrel-straightener had cut small-arms production there by 360 rifles a month. There was no one to replace him, unless from the army. But such pleas had little effect. In October, 1864, new conscription regulations forced the supply bureaus to return one-fifth of their detailed men to the army.

Even when details were made, there was no guarantee of permanence, for they had to be renewed at frequent intervals. Renewals were denied during periods of extreme emergency, such as the Wilderness campaign in 1864. Even some men detailed by the Secretary of War were pressed into conscript camps by overzealous enrolling officers who were anxious to keep the camps filled so that they, themselves, would not have to go to the front. These press gangs were so efficient that the Chief of Ordnance found his department with more machines than he had men to run them in late 1864. Quite a reversal of things from 1861.

There were even problems with unskilled labor. Not many unskilled white men were available for duty in supply plants or depots, and those who were had proved unfit for field service and, after being enrolled for limited duty, found their way to supply installations. The main reliance for unskilled labor was upon the slaves.

Slaves constituted a large body of manpower which was not allowed to serve directly in the armed forces. But there were things which these noncitizens could do for the war effort. If they did the menial jobs of the army, such as digging trenches, building fortifications, driving teams, and constructing public buildings, many able-bodied white men could be released for line duty. Slaves were useful, too, to government contractors, even performing skilled work in some private iron-works.

Slaves had to come from somewhere. The usual policy was to hire them from their owners. When, as all too frequently happened, owners proved unwilling to hire their property to government agencies, slaves were impressed. Impressment could not be resorted to by all private contractors, and these had to raise the rates for hired labor. None of these things helped the condition of Confederate finances or raised the reputation of the government. So it was that the labor situation was rarely satisfactory.

Too little attention has been given to the general subject of labor in the Confederacy. Some special studies have been made, such as Bell I. Wiley's excellent *Southern Negroes, 1861–1865,* but the field is still open for investigation. It might well prove extremely revealing to a student of Confederate economics.

The virtually insurmountable problems of procurement facing the Confederate supply services forced them to makeshift substitutes of many sorts. For example, the Quartermaster Department, continually hampered by the growing scarcity of cloth for such things as cavalry saddle blankets, successfully experimented with a moss-filled substitute. The shortage of leather drove the same department to wooden-soled, canvas-topped brogans, which seemed to please everybody but the infantrymen. The Ordnance Bureau, with all sorts of shortages hindering its operations, was perhaps the most makeshift-minded of all the departments: iron was made to do for bronze in artillery manufacture; whisky stills were cut up for copper; and lead was taken from battlefields, window weights, and water mains. These are only a few examples of procurement ingenuity displayed by the various supply branches—and ingenuity was about all that kept them going after a couple of years.

Procurement was but one phase of logistics. If any gradation be possible, transportation ranked next in importance, and, like everything else, it also was a matter of money. It was a matter of a lot of other things, too—decaying railroads, emaciated animals, and ramshackle wagons and caissons. Of the money problem mention has already been made, but of the railroads something more needs to be said.

Railroads were the big new factor in logistics. It was the railroad that made possible the gigantic operations of modern war. The Confederacy had serious problems with its railroads—problems generally well known, and now much clearer as a result of the recent work of Robert C. Black III in his *Railroads of the Confederacy.*

These problems were first studied by Charles W. Ramsdell, whose article on "The Confederate

Government and the Railroads," in the *American Historical Review* (1916–17), was a pioneer work in the new field of Confederate logistics. As Ramsdell and Black have shown, Rebel railroads were cursed with many gauges, no new equipment, few building and repair facilities, small amounts of track, and the selfishness of some of the companies. More than this, the government stood at fault in compounding the chaos of rail transportation. No coherent policy was worked out for the efficient management of the roads. There was much talk of a railroad bureau, under the Quartermaster General (there was even a director of railroad transportation), but the Confederacy could never quite bring itself to efficiently organize and run the railroads, though some War Department regulation was authorized by law. The problems of the various lines grew increasingly serious. Some government efforts were made to aid individual companies, but without too much success.

As Black concludes, it is remarkable that so much was accomplished by the Confederate rail lines, in view of the problems they faced. Trains, of a sort, were still creaking over patched and uneven roadbeds at the very end. Essentially, though, the railroads might have been much more effectively used. A priority plan was never really introduced which would have aided in getting the most essential supplies to the area of greatest need. The conclusion is inescapable that this new dimension in rapid transit was not used to best advantage.

Some reasons suggest themselves at once. One problem was the very newness of railroads as a military asset. No one quite knew how to use them, but the Quartermaster Department, as well as the other bureaus, kept experimenting with new plans and schemes for better use of the roads. They were learning. Then, too, some supply officers in charge of rail transportation used their authority for their own benefit. Suspiciously large amounts of private freight always seemed to find space on the trains while government goods went begging.

The railroads of the Union were far more potent as a weapon of war than were those of the South. The North had so many more miles of track, so many more building and repair facilities, and a much better plan of railroad control than ever existed south of Mason and Dixon's line. The South found itself forced to greater reliance upon horses for military transport, and, at first, horses were plentiful. After all, the South was the great area of horsemanship, where horsebreeding was refined to a science and where a man's knowledge of horseflesh was accepted as part of his culture. Virginia boasted some of the finest breeds and best stables, but Louisiana was not to be counted out, and neither was Kentucky. Nor, indeed, could any of the Southern states be considered completely dismounted.

Kentucky, though, could not be relied upon. She longed for an impossible neutrality and finally was occupied by Lincoln's troops. So it was the rest of the South that would carry the burden of supplying the horses for the Confederate cavalry, the artillery, and all of the wagons and ambulances required by the army—and the navy, too, for that matter. These other states served well as sources for a time.

It is certainly a matter for debate whether or not the Confederate cavalry, during the first years of the war, was the best the world had ever seen. Not only did it symbolize the chivalric and cavalier South, it also became a new element in war. The Confederate cavalry, with such leaders as Ashby, Forrest, Stuart, and Wheeler, was the forerunner of the blitzkrieg—employing the tactics of strike, run, strike again. All the Federal cavalry could do, mounted on heavier, plodding, horses was trail along at a respectful distance and froth at the mouth. But then there came a terrible change.

By the middle of 1863, the Yankee cavalrymen were not running or following along behind any longer. They were attacking. Mounted now on good, lithe, western horses, the men made up in stamina what their leaders lacked in native daring. At the same time, the Confederate cavalry horses were growing thin and worn with hard riding, for forage had become scarce and so had replacements.

Some field artillery had to be eliminated from Lee's army because horses, in 1864, could not be found to pull it. What horses remained for the artillery were bags of bones whose appearance earned the sympathy of Lee's hardened skeletons. Regimental wagon transportation was curtailed in all the field armies, and the Medical Corps had to make do with fewer ambulances.

Again it was Ramsdell who first studied the problem of horses as a factor in the Confederacy's decline. His article in the *American Historical Review* (1929–30) on "General Robert E. Lee's Horse Supply, 1862–65," pointed out causes of starvation. The emaciation of the animals was most marked in the areas of active campaigning, where both armies had foraged widely and taken all the available food. The strict necessity for bringing up food and munitions from the rear made it impossible for the Quartermaster Department to ship adequate amounts of forage for the animals. The condition of the railroads was not always the reason —the haphazard transportation plan of the Quartermaster Department sometimes contributed to the shortage of supplies.

The growing weakness of horse transportation was complicated by the fact that new sources of horseflesh were hard to find. The contracting borders of the Confederacy left less and less area from which to draw. The remount service of the Quartermaster Department found it increasingly difficult to find replacements for horses expended or worn out in campaigning, and the same problem afflicted the individual cavalryman, striving to provide his own mount. Horses captured from the enemy offered some hope for sustaining the supply, but could not be counted on indefinitely. What was true of the cavalry was also true of all other services depending on horses.

Transportation in general was a problem to be handled by the Quartermaster Department, and this agency worked hard at the job. As the examples cited indicate, however, the basic problems were never solved. In a way, this was probably the greatest single failure of the department—certainly some of the other supply bureaus took this view. The objection of most of the other services was that the Quartermaster Department had complete control over transportation. This they felt to be wrong. Who could know better how to transport medicine than the Medical Corps, for instance? Each bureau felt its own particular needs to be far greater than those of any of the others, and priority should be given to its shipments. Generally, and quite naturally, what priority existed went to quartermaster shipments and this did nothing to further interservice harmony.

Such harmony was further retarded by the heavy-handed use of impressing authority by the different agencies. All of the bureaus had this authority, and they extended its use into the field of transportation, invading the preserve of the Quartermaster Department. On occasion the Commissary Department would impress all the freight cars in a given locality for the shipment of foodstuffs, leaving nothing for the other services to use. Such selfishness did not always work, for the Quartermaster Department might, at the same time, impress all the locomotives, leaving the commissary cars high and dry.

This may have been funny to the officers vying with each other, but such episodes were far from laughable. This sort of thing meant that somewhere in the chain of command basic logistical organization was lacking. Too much authority had been indiscriminately delegated and consequently too little got done.

The Quartermaster Department ought not to be too severely condemned for the pattern of chaos established in the transportation of Confederate supplies, for despite the vicious conflict of authority and lack of clear-cut command, supplies did get to the armies.

That was the objective of all the activity of the bureaus—to get the supplies to the field forces. Distribution at the operational level was largely an army problem, involving the staff-department representatives with the separate armies.

The chief quartermaster, chief commissary, or chief ordnance officer of each army was expected to provide enough supplies for the army. He was expected, too, to see that these supplies did not run short as the army campaigned. The careful army commander gave his chief staff officers some idea of what was going on. Supplies could then be ordered from depots in time to anticipate shortages. The depot was the intermediate point between the army and the procurement of supplies. It was the great "warehouse" of the field army.

Cloth, for instance, might be obtained by the Quartermaster Department from North Carolina textile mills, shipped by rail (if trains could be found) to the Richmond quartermaster shops, where it would be made into uniforms which were held in the Richmond depot subject to the order of Lee's chief quartermaster. The Richmond depot was principally concerned with Lee's army—largely because of geography and the importance of his forces. The same was generally true of the Richmond depots of the other staff agencies. The capital was Lee's base of supplies.

The depot system had many advantages. It tended to centralize the accumulation of supplies, made it possible to stockpile items not immediately needed, and simplified the distribution problem. As the transportation system became less efficient, more and more depots appeared. The reason is obvious: small depots fairly close to supply sources, as well as to field armies, took much strain off the railroads.

The depot, or arsenal, commander was a man of large powers and equally large responsibilities, depending on the size of his installation. He had to be sure that he had enough supplies on hand to meet all supply requests (requisitions) which might come to him. This made it essential that he should have considerable power to request additional supplies directly from the chiefs of supply departments. His discretion was trusted, else he would not —theoretically—have had the job. If the distribution area of his depot were large, he might have several subordinates, whose tasks would include keeping accurate inventories of stock on hand, bookkeeping, labor supervision, and transport management.

The commander himself acted as a sort of store manager. He supervised the activities of all his subordinate officers and men, received requisitions and assumed responsibility for failure to comply with them. Once a requisition came in from a field force, the depot commander got busy. He first checked to see if the requisition came from within his area, made certain that the required supplies were in stock, and then ordered them sent to the army's supply point. In emergencies he usually had authority to call on other depots to aid him in furnishing items which he did not have, and he could impress transportation, as well as labor. But once the supplies were in transit, his responsibility supposedly ended.

Actually, the diligent depot commander was

concerned with his shipment until he was certain it had reached its destination. The run-of-the-mill officer would be satisfied with a quartermaster receipt for the shipment; if the quartermaster did not deliver, the depot was protected by the bill of lading. Conscientious officers, who wanted to be sure that their consignments reached the front, would send along special agents with the shipment to insure speedy and safe delivery. Such officers rose rapidly in rank and influence.

Such officers also made things much easier for army staff officers. The responsibility of the army officers began when the supplies reached the army supply dumps. The chief quartermaster, chief commissary, chief ordnance officer—all of the army's chief staff officers—receipted for delivery to the army and apportioned the total amount of food, stores, and equipment to the various corps; then the corps supply officers funneled the supplies down to division level, where the process was repeated. Division, then brigade, staffs took charge of the stores, and at the end of the line the sergeants took final delivery, issuing food, clothing, and equipment to the men in the ranks. By the time supplies got to the sergeants for final distribution they had traveled a long and hard road. The sergeants were important men in the supply chain.

The whole process would have been impossible without a coherent, workable chain of command in all of the supply bureaus. The chain of command in the field has been explained, but everything depended on how well organized at the command level were the bureaus themselves.

The chiefs of the supply bureaus were most concerned with an over-all view of logistics. Their task was to see that the whole business of supply from procurement to distribution went smoothly. This task could be performed only by an efficient administrative organization, and for the most part the bureaus had such organization. Take the Ordnance Bureau as an example: The Chief of Ordnance had the over-all command of the bureau, but under his immediate eye were deputies charged with special phases of the Chief's work. There was the Deputy Chief of Ordnance, a lieutenant colonel, who was, in effect, an administrative assistant. He shouldered much of the direct correspondence with ordnance officers in the field, kept up with the running needs of various armies and with the needs of the arsenals, armories, depots, and ordnance shops. He was able to tell the Chief of Ordnance of weaknesses in the bureau's capacity to do its job and generally knew what was going on in the whole bureau. Naturally, if the need arose, he could step in as Chief of Ordnance.

In addition to the deputy chief, there was a moderate office staff consisting of several lesser officers charged with keeping track of appropriations, expenses, and special technical functions. The command of the bureau was not wholly centered in the head office, because the general condition of the Confederacy, as has been shown, demanded some decentralization of activities. The Superintendent of Laboratories, a scientist in uniform, was stationed in Macon, Georgia, in the Confederate States Central Laboratories. The Chief of Ordnance delegated to him complete command over all laboratories of the bureau. In addition, he had general supervision of research and development.

Also in Macon was the Superintendent of Armories. This man had wide knowledge of armory operations and supervised the activities of all such installations insofar as technique and operational procedure went.

Naturally, the most important field officers of the bureau were the army ordnance officers. They held rank (usually lieutenant colonel) and prestige equal to that of arsenal commanders. Attached to the staff of the general commanding the army, they could correspond directly with Richmond and requisition supplies directly from the depots. Unfortunately, there was no clear understanding of the command relationship of the bureau to the army ordnance officers. The question arose repeatedly whether or not the Chief of Ordnance in Richmond could issue orders concerning the ordnance stores of an army directly to the chief army ordnance officer, or whether his orders would first have to pass through the general commanding that army.

JEFFERSON DAVIS

This bothersome problem rankled for the duration of the war.

Then there were the individual arsenal, armory, depot, and shop commanders, with more limited command responsibility. Under the general supervision of the head office, each had charge of the operation and output of his own installation. Farther down the scale, post ordnance officers had charge of the storage and issue of ordnance stores at posts, camps, and stations.

This same organization, with essentially the same problems, was the pattern for all the supply bureaus. One significant variation, according to regulations at any rate, appeared in the Commissary Department. Here the setup was similar to Ordnance, with the addition of an extra cog in the machine, a state commissary officer, who had general charge of procurement in his state.

Such an exhausting table of organization points clearly to a growing bureaucracy and to endless miles of red tape. As the war progressed, however, and all the bureaus learned by experience, there was a clear trend apparent in their operations. Forced by the transportation system into decentralizing depot operations, the bureaus nonetheless moved more toward unified command. Certainly much authority was delegated by the chiefs of the bureaus to field officers—nothing would have been done without this—but the authority delegated was restricted to operational matters; the over-all logistical planning was rarely done except at Richmond. The bureau chiefs learned a great deal about centralizing command functions as time passed. The result was spectacular. Most of the bureau heads could boast of smoothly running agencies and brief the Secretary of War, with little advance notice, on the general condition of their departments.

The tragedy was that there was no unifying influence above individual bureaus. With organizations as efficient as were most of the supply services, what might a Chief of Logistics, for instance, have accomplished?

An official of this sort could possibly have done more than co-ordinate army supply efforts. He might have made more harmonious and profitable the relations between army and navy bureaus. The navy had the same kind of supply agencies that the army had: there was a Bureau of Ordnance and Hydrography, an Office of Provisions and Clothing, and an Office of Medicine and Surgery. All too frequently the army and navy agents worked at cross purposes, vied with each other for scarce items, and outbid one another for skilled labor. Far more could have been accomplished had the two services co-ordinated their procurement and transportation operations. Again the lack of a directing hand was painfully apparent.

In only one instance during the war was there an

attempt at what might be called a combined logistical operation. Blockade-running was probably the best organized and administered of all supply functions. Not at first—but as time went on, the system matured and was refined into an extremely efficient business.

As far as the administration was concerned, blockade-running should never have happened. Early views of the Confederate State Department reflected the legalistic twist in the President's thinking. Davis wanted to convince Europe that the Federal blockade was a sieve, that countless ships reached Southern ports with no trouble. This idea, of course, precluded for some time the Confederate government's participation in any blockade-running activities.

But foreign sources of supply were vital. Most particularly to such agencies as the Ordnance Bureau, for the South was so woefully deficient in industry. Arms, machinery, powder, artillery— everything—could be purchased in England and Europe. And until home production could be put on its feet, foreign supplies were essential. The same attitude was held by the Medical Department, equally without home sources of its needs. So these two agencies entered into blockade-running.

It was not easy. Strong opposition came from the President, but grudging approval was finally won. Davis was made to see the desperate situation of these bureaus, and he could close an eye to their doings, provided they kept their trade out of the limelight.

The Chief of Ordnance deserves credit for getting the Confederate government involved in running the blockade. He bought some blockade-runners, five of them, and these made a phenomenal number of successful trips through the Federal patrols. His operations began in 1861, but it was not until 1863 that he got any real co-operation from the Secretary of War.

In the intervening time he had to set up his own system and arrange all the details of payment, pur-chasing, and transport. He did well. To Europe were dispatched ordnance procurement agents, along with some medical agents. These men, armed with whatever credit a promise to send cotton would gain, toured England, France, Prussia, and other parts of the Continent seeking companies willing to sell war materiel to the South. When possible they contracted for the manufacture of ar-tillery, small arms, and other necessary items, such as armory and arsenal machinery and medicines.

Cotton was purchased by the Ordnance Bureau, put on board the bureau's runners and sent abroad. Once in England, it usually found its way to the firm of Saul Isaac, Campbell and Company, or Fraser, Trenholm and Company. These import-export brokerage houses sold the cotton, deducted a commission, and credited the proceeds to the ordnance and medical accounts. They were willing to extend credit, even when cotton was slow to come, and without them nothing could have been accomplished.

It was confidently expected at first that home manufacturing, plus foreign recognition of the Confederacy, would soon make blockade-running unnecessary, but these things did not happen. Domestic industry never was developed to its full potential—partially because there was so little to start with—and, of course, recognition was denied.

So blockade-running grew in importance. And as it did, it became more and more necessary to expand the system, to organize it, and to make it a part of the logistical pattern of the Confederacy. This required more centralized, unified direction of all blockade-running efforts.

More money and cotton came from the Secretary of War, along with authority to build and rent large depots for storage of supplies in Bermuda and Nassau. Authority was also given to engage government space on blockade-runners. Other supply bureaus became interested, and the whole business became so hectic that the Ordnance Bureau asked for help.

Then, in 1864, the Bureau of Foreign Supplies was set up, with general supervision of all government blockade-running activities. This was just what was needed. The bureau had sufficient authority to allot shipping space and cotton to the bureaus most needing them and to administer all phases of the foreign purchasing program. As a result, real co-ordination of effort was achieved.

The Secretary of State directed his commercial agents in the British West Indies to lend aid to blockade-running efforts. The Secretary of the Treasury helped in obtaining cotton for shipment to the purchasing agents abroad. Even private blockade-running firms, assured compensation in cotton by the Bureau of Foreign Supplies, yielded precious space. The bureau had authority, had this space not been made available, to force private companies to ship government cargoes.

The affairs on the European side were not well handled. Before the Bureau of Foreign Supplies took over, almost every state, plus the commander of the Trans-Mississippi Department, had a purchasing agent in Europe. So did some of the army and navy supply bureaus not concerned with the few government-owned blockade-runners. Chaos resulted. There were so many different Confederate agents wandering around that no one could keep up with them. They competed with Federal agents, but they also competed with each other.

There had to be a stop to all this wasted motion. Some order was achieved after a special agent went to Europe in 1863 to administer the Erlanger Loan. Colin J. McRae took all financial transactions into his own hands and supervised all contracts and payments for all Confederate purchasing. He was the one most aware of how many different Rebels were running around loose in Europe, and, seconded by the Chief of Ordnance, he successfully urged the War Department to set up something like a Bureau of Foreign Supplies. He also effectively urged the purchase of more blockade-runners and the more efficient management of the business end of procurement in England and France. Had McRae gone to England earlier, blockade-running might have altered the course of the war.

Convincing statistics are available to indicate the success of blockade-running. These results were the direct outgrowth of intelligent planning and effective co-ordination, and no other major effort made by the Confederacy was as well organized and administered. True, the Federal blockade grew tighter and tighter, and the system of evading the blockade did not solve the South's supply problems. Suffice it to say that defeat might have come much sooner to the Confederacy without blockade-running. Final failure was not because of some inherent flaw in its organization—the system died with the Confederate armies.

Why was blockade-running so well administered? Why was co-operation of all branches of the government possible in this area when it could not be achieved elsewhere? There are some possible answers. Blockade-running was an activity which vitally concerned all of the supply bureaus—and consequently the whole government. All agencies were in measure dependent on the swift little ships darting from Bermuda to Wilmington or from Nassau to Charleston, and from Cuba to the Gulf ports.

So possibly interbureau jealousy was never a factor in blockade-running. They all had to help each other, otherwise the system would not have paid off. Possibly, too, the fact that blockade-running was a new element in logistics, even newer than the railroad, had something to do with it. Nothing of this sort had ever been tried in modern war on so large a scale; the organization was new, the method was new, and the very fact of inter-service co-operation was new. Since there was no precedent for it, there was no pile of red tape, no volume of "doctrine," as it would be called today, to draw on. Starting from scratch, it was comparatively easy to see that absolute co-operation was essential. The men charged with organizing blockade-running had something to do with it, too. The Chief of Ordnance, who first gave some direction to the business, clearly recognized the need for co-ordination, so the principle was present from the beginning of the system.

Others associated with the administration of the Confederate end of blockade-running were not stupid. John Slidell, Henry Hotze, Benjamin, McRae, and even Davis saw the problem. All of the supply officers recognized the need for co-operation, although they had been unable to cut through bales of regulations to achieve it in their regular bureau operations. Once there was a chance for a combined logistical effort, unhampered by artificial obstacles, they knew what ought to be done and did it. This fact alone indicates a degree of competence on the part of the Confederate supply chiefs for which they have not received credit.

Blockade-running was the one area of logistics in which command responsibilities were properly understood and accepted. It marked the high point of Confederate logistical efficiency. But in other supply activities efficiency was growing.

All of the bureaus concerned with getting supplies and equipment to the troops had started the war with loose ideas of organization. They were not unique—the thinking of all military men followed the same pattern. War, remember, was largely personal. Offices could be small and most of the tasks of the supply bureaus could be done by few officers with slight direction from the Secretary of War.

Small thinking and small organizations were as outdated as small war. Big armies, big troop movements, and big battles jolted the old supply system into new shapes. New ways of supplying en masse had to be found in the midst of fighting. So many functions had to be performed which had never been dreamed of before, and this is what started the red-tape ball rolling. In order to do all these new things, while continuing to do the old ones, the supply departments had to create new offices, get more men, and build more installations.

The expanded bureaus were administered in a simple and clear way. The basic organization of the offices would not be changed, but new offices were added and some authority was delegated. There was no time to work out a better plan. Sometimes this resulted in vaguely defined authority, competition on the part of officers of the same department, and other errors. No central agency to mastermind logistical planning was ever set up, though it may well be that the next best thing was done. Each supply chief assumed greater executive duties, making his department look more and more like a modern corporation. Experience taught these Confederates some valuable lessons about business enterprise, and never was native American ingenuity more effectively displayed.

The system, such as it was, worked. And had other things been equal, it was probably workable enough to have lasted. All of which is to say that there was nothing fatally wrong with the organization of the individual supply departments, although some were better organized than others. The big mistakes were made at higher levels.

There was a lot about Confederate logistics that needed improvement. There may well have been too much of the spirit of business enterprise present on some occasions, and too much competition was not a good thing for the war effort. Interservice jealousies, plus the empire-building attitudes displayed by some supply officers, did nothing to win the war.

Patriotism sometimes lost its appeal when matched against the drawing power of money—even Confederate money. Almost all the services of supply had speculators in their midst who sold goods illegally or who impressed more than they reported to their superiors, using the remainder as a nest egg for themselves. This sort of thing sounds impossible to many modern Confederates who seem to feel that there never was a purer, more stainless nation on the face of the earth. Naturally, dishonesty appeared in the Confederacy, for Confederates were human. The fact that they were human and displayed all the human weaknesses and foibles only adds to their accomplishments.

But these weaknesses made for a lot of wasted motion. With a solid unifying direction to whip all the erring elements of supply into line, Confederate logistics might well have been completely successful. And had all of the economic and human resources of the South been managed for a total war effort, the Rebels could have won the war. From where should the directing influence have come? Since supervision of administration was the President's function, he should have provided the necessary co-ordination. But perhaps his earlier experience, both as a professionally trained soldier and as

Secretary of War, immobilized him as the one to do the job. There is some evidence that he was not wholly unaware of what needed to be done. His experiments with unified army command show him to have been groping in the direction of a chief of staff, as well as a general staff organization, which might have solved the logistical problem.

Confederate logisticians were forced by circumstances to make do with what they had. The same was true of the President. In the daily urgency of war, he could not afford sweeping organizational changes, but had to move toward a modern command system slowly, carefully. Logistical planning was something new—never before had it been necessary to plan for such a mammoth effort. So everything was an experiment. There was no time for the careful development of theories—these had to follow after practical trials.

Attempts to solve problems posed by total war and mass logistics led Confederate logisticians, as well as strategists, inevitably away from the loose, personal administrative and command organization and inevitably toward concentration of command authority and a more modern staff. The South lost the war before modernization took place or before a general staff of the German sort was created. But even so, the Confederacy was able to organize and direct a massive war effort for four years. This was no small achievement.

The achievement is even more impressive when

weighed against all the odds. The steadfast heroism of the Confederate soldier has long been the subject of deserved admiration. But it is time that some of that admiration went to those unsung men who made it possible for the soldier to do his job.

Confederate war planners have been criticized for failing to mobilize all the resources of the South. In his book *A History of the Southern Confederacy,* Clement Eaton accepts the idea that "the cause was lost because there was no Wisdom in Congress and no Public Virtue among the People," implying that with more wisdom and virtue the South's resources would have been efficiently handled. Perhaps these remarks could be extended. The cause may have been lost because there was not wisdom enough to recognize the beginning of a new era and not enough understanding of total war to evolve a command and logistical system adequate to the job at hand. Hindsight makes it easy to attack the Confederate leaders, but also compels a sympathy with them. Considering the split personality of the South—tradition versus modernization; ideals versus reality—Rebel leaders made quite a fight.

Possibly, then, the factor that most damaged the Confederacy was this split personality—an inability to reconcile two strong tendencies. Total war brought the South closer and closer to strong central government, with the inevitable emphasis on centralization of administration and military command. At the same time the traditional state rights attitude of localism, or decentralization, continued strong. These two urges constantly pulled against one another. The trend toward limited centralization could be seen in the changing management of the supply bureaus and in Davis' experiments with unified command. The trend toward decentralization continued in the efforts of Governors Brown and Vance to resist strong government and in the failure of the President and his cabinet to centralize control of the nation's war effort at the top. All of which points to the idea that the South may have been wrecked by decentralized centralization.

Bibliographical Note

IN AN INCISIVE and stimulating short essay entitled "The Place of the American Civil War in the Evolution of War," *Army Quarterly,* XXVI (1933), 316–25, Major General J. F. C. Fuller ventured the opinion that the issue of strategic command was basic in the history of the Civil War. This article seems to have created no appreciable reaction either in England or the United States. Not until recently, as a matter of fact, has the subject of command in a broad sense attracted the attention of Civil War students. In 1952 T. Harry Williams published *Lincoln and His Generals* (New York, 1952), which views the Union President as the leader of a national war effort and discusses his fight to organize an effective modern command system. Beyond these two works little has been done on the subject. Virtually nothing has been done on the Confederate side, save the military studies of Douglas Southall Freeman.

Some general books on the Confederacy point up special phases of the story. Among the most helpful general accounts are E. Merton Coulter's *The Confederate States of America, 1861–1865* (Baton Rouge, 1950), Clement Eaton's *A History of the Southern Confederacy* (New York, 1954), and Robert S. Henry's *The Story of the Confederacy* (New York, 1931), though none of these deals specifically with the idea of command in a total war.

A good number of special accounts contribute to the general outline—so many, in fact, that only a select group will be listed here.

The early organization of both the Union and Confederate

REBEL BRASS

War Departments is interestingly treated by Brigadier General William H. Carter in "The War Department: Military Administration," *Scribner's Magazine,* XXXIII (1903), 661–73. Also useful for the early history of staff organization is Lieutenant Colonel J. D. Hittle, *The Military Staff: Its History and Development* (Harrisburg, Pa., 1949).

For the special problem of manpower and its relation to organization, Albert B. Moore, *Conscription and Conflict in the Confederacy* (New York, 1924), is extremely good. This same volume sheds some light on the labor problem as a whole.

The question of Confederate civilian administration has received wide attention. Among the works which proved most valuable in evaluating Jefferson Davis as President and commander in chief were Davis' own *Rise and Fall of the Confederate Government* (2 vols., New York, 1881); Clifford Dowdey, *Experiment in Rebellion* (New York, 1946); H. J. Eckenrode, *Jefferson Davis: President of the South* (New York, 1923); Burton J. Hendrick, *Statesmen of the Lost Cause: Jefferson Davis and His Cabinet* (Boston, 1939); Joseph E. Johnston, *Narrative of Military Operations Directed During the Late War Between the States* (New York, 1874); Rembert W. Patrick, *Jefferson Davis and His Cabinet* (Baton Rouge, 1944); Dunbar Rowland (ed.), *Jefferson Davis, Constitutionalist: His Letters, Papers and Speeches* (10 vols., Jackson, Miss., 1923).

Two additional works shed light on Davis' relations with his cabinet: Joseph T. Durkin, *Stephen R. Mallory: Confederate Navy Chief* (Chapel Hill, 1954), and Robert Douthat Meade, *Judah P. Benjamin: Confederate Statesman* (New York, 1943).

The Confederate Congress revealed a great deal about itself. The *Journal of the Congress of the Confederate States of America, 1861–1865* (7 vols., Washington, 1904–1905), is a mountain of information. Equally valuable are the debates of the Congress, which were reported in Richmond newspapers. These are now being reprinted in the *Southern Historical Society Papers.* The first installment appeared in Volume XLIV (1923), and the series will be complete with the publication of two final volumes.

The whole subject of state rights in the wartime South is touched upon in countless sources. The most well-known, and most valuable, is Frank L. Owsley, *State Rights in the Confederacy* (Chicago, 1925).

In the area of logistics the sources are numerous. Clement Eaton in his new *History of the Southern Confederacy* devotes an excellent chapter to "The Logistics of the Gray Army"—the first general survey of the topic. Confederate governmental efforts to manage procurement and control the economy are considered in Robert C. Black III, *The Railroads of the Confederacy* (Chapel Hill, 1952); Louise B. Hill, *State Socialism in the Confederate States of America,* in *Southern Sketches,* Series I, No. 9 (Charlottesville, 1936); Ella Lonn, *Salt as a Factor in the Confederacy* (New York, 1933); James L. Nichols, "Confederate Quartermaster Operations in the Trans-Mississippi Department" (M.A. thesis, University of Texas), and the same author, "The Confederate Engineers" (Ph.D. dissertation, University of Texas); Frank L. Owsley, *King Cotton Diplomacy* (Chicago, 1931); Charles W. Ramsdell, "The Confederate Government and the Railroads," *American Historical Review,* XXII (1916–17), 794–810; Ramsdell, "The Control of Manufacturing by the Confederate Government," *Mississippi Valley Historical Review,* VIII (1921–22), 231–49; Ramsdell, "General Robert E. Lee's Horse Supply, 1862–1865," *American Historical Review,* XXXV (1929–30), 758–77; and again Ramsdell, *Behind the Lines in the Southern Confederacy* (Baton Rouge, 1944)—a brilliant series of essays in the social-economic history of the Confederacy; John C. Schwab, *The Confederate States of America, 1861–1865. A Financial and Industrial History of the South During the Civil War* (New Haven, 1913, c. 1901); Frank E. Vandiver, "The Shelby Iron Company in the Civil War: A Study of a Confederate Industry," *Alabama Review,* I (1948), 13–26, 111–27, 203–17; Vandiver, *Ploughshares Into Swords:*

Josiah Gorgas and Confederate Ordnance (Austin, 1952); Bell I. Wiley, *The Plain People of the Confederacy* (Baton Rouge, 1943).

Blockade-running is a specialized topic. There are legions of memoirs, journals, and romances in print illustrating all the various facets of the story. The accounts upon which the discussion in the text is based include Francis B. C. Bradlee, *Blockade Running During the Civil War and the Effect of Land and Water Transportation on the Confederacy* (Salem, Mass., 1925); Caleb Huse, *The Supplies for the Confederate Army* (Boston, 1904); Owsley, *King Cotton Diplomacy* (the classic in the field); Samuel B. Thompson, *Confederate Purchasing Operations Abroad* (Chapel Hill, 1935); Vandiver, *Confederate Blockade Running Through Bermuda, 1861–1865: Letters and Cargo Manifests* (Austin, 1947).

Obviously many other sources are available which bear on the subject of this book. It is impossible here to list them all. This bibliographical note is designed to be merely suggestive—not by any means definitive. The books included serve to indicate the wide range of approaches which may be used in studying the problem of Confederate command.

Index

Adjutant General, C.S.A., 84; and efforts to co-ordinate military operations, 21
Adjutant General, U.S.A., 84
Agriculture, in Confederacy, 13, 14, 82
Alabama, 20, 36, 43, 44, 57, 60; industry in, 15; ordnance plants in, 15
Alabama, C.S.S., 68, 72
American Revolution, 41, 79
Ammunition, supplies of, for C.S. Armies, 85–86; amount consumed in battle, 86
Anti-Semitism, in Confederacy, 45
Appomattox, Va., 19
Army, Confederate States, 72, 73, 74; organization of, 4; dispersal of, by Davis, 26; and combined operations, 72; logistical chain of command in, 110
Army of Northern Virginia (Confederate), 30, 31, 32, 104, 105, 108
Army of the Potomac (Federal), 51
Army of Tennessee (Confederate), 32, 33, 36, 59
Army, United States, 12, 84
Arsenals, Confederate, commanders of, and logistics, 108–10, 113
Ashby, Gen. Turner, C.S.A., 104
Atlanta, Georgia, 36
Attorney General, Confederate, 45

Baton Rouge, Louisiana, 72
Beauregard, Gen. P. G. T., C.S.A., 28, 29, 33; commands Military Division of the West, 36–37

INDEX

Benjamin, Judah P., 45, 120; evaluation of, as Confederate Secretary of War, 45–48; relations with Jefferson Davis, 46; and threatened resignation of Stonewall Jackson, 46–47; and loss of Roanoke Island, 47; becomes Confederate Secretary of State, 47
Bermuda, 117, 120
Big Bethel, Va., Battle of, 49
Black, Robert C., III, 101, 102
Blockade, 8, 85, 115, 119
Blockade-runners, 65
Blockade-running, 56, 70, 86–87, 117; a combined logistical operation, 115; organization and administration of, 115–21; evaluation of, 119–21; command responsibility for, 121
Bragg, Gen. Braxton, C.S.A., 28, 29, 33, 34, 52, 57, 58, 59; Kentucky campaign of, 86
Breckinridge, John C., Confederate Secretary of War, 63
British West Indies, 118
Bronze, 86, 101
Brown, Joseph E., Governor of Georgia, 39, 126
Buchanan, Franklin, C.S.N., 12
Bulloch, James D., Confederate Naval Agent in England, 65
Bureau of Conscription, Confederate, 11, 97

Calhoun, John C., 55
Campbell, Saul Isaac, & Co., 116
Cape Fear River, 10
Cavalry, Confederate, 104–106
Cavalry, Federal, 104
Charleston, S.C., 120; Democratic Convention in, 44
Chief of Ordnance, C.S.A., 84, 91
Chief of Ordnance, U.S.A., 80, 84
Clausewitz, xvii, 7
Cloth, 108; shortage of, in Confederacy, 100
Clothing, for Confederate Army, 90, 94

INDEX

INDEX

Davis, Jefferson (*Continued*)
views on centralization, 19; ideas of, on army command, 23; in Mexican War, 24; in U.S. House of Representatives, 24; in U.S. Senate, 24; as U.S. Secretary of War, 24–25; evaluation of, as leader of Confederate war effort, 24–43; compared with Lincoln, 25; and rules of war, 27; and foreign purchasing, 28; relations with Gen. Lee, 29–30; attempts to create unified command, 35–36; and delegation of authority, 37, 40, 42; relations with Confederate Congress, 37–38, 76–77; relations with state governors, 39; as politician, 40; his own Secretary of War, 40, 43; not a revolutionary, 41; views on Confederate Secretaries of War, 44; relations with J. P. Benjamin, 46; and threatened resignation of Gen. Stonewall Jackson, 47; appoints Benjamin Secretary of State, 47–48; dictates policy of War Department, 48; relations with G. W. Randolph, 49–54; concern of, for west, 51; changing views on functions of Secretary of War, 54; relations with J. A. Seddon, 54–62; controversy with J. E. Johnston, 58; relations with S. R. Mallory, 63–74; fails to give executive leadership to Congress, 76; isolated from Congress, 76; characterizes war effort, 82; and co-ordination of logistics, 87; views on blockade-running, 115; a co-ordinator of logistical operations, 123–24; and modern command system, 124
Department of the West (Confederate), 56, 57
Depots, supply, in Confederacy, 108–109; commanders of, and logistics, 108–10, 113; and distribution of Army supplies, 108–10
Democratic Party, 44, 63
Donald, David, xv, xix; on Civil War historiography, xv–xvi
Drury's Bluff, Virginia, 73
Durkin, Joseph T., 64

Eaton, Clement, 125
Economic warfare, 68
Economy, Confederate, 65, 88–126; a factor in strategy and

[134]

INDEX

command, 8, 12–16; price schedules, 62, 93; taxation, 76; inflation, 77, 89, 93, 95; and national war effort, 81, 82–126; affected by blockade, 85
Engineer Corps, C.S.A., 84
England, 65, 116, 119
Erlanger Loan, 77, 118
Europe, 65, 115, 118, 119

First Manassas, Battle of, 33
Florida, 63, 64
Florida, C.S.S., 68
Food, in Confederacy, 90, 93
Foreign Supplies, Bureau of, C.S.A., 86, 118, 119; supervises blockade-running activities, 117
Forrest, Gen. Nathan B., C.S.A., 104; and modern war, 12
France, 116, 119
Franklin, Tenn., Battle of, 37
Fraser, Trenholm & Co., 116

General Staff, 124; functions of, 7; need for, in Confederacy, 18, 21
Geography, helps to splinter Confederacy, 20; affects strategy and military administration, 8–10, 34, 81
Georgia, 37, 39, 57, 60; ordnance plants in, 15
Gloire, French ironclad, 69
Gorgas, Gen. Josiah, C.S.A., 7, 53, 64, 84, 98, 99, 111, 112, 119, 120; buys blockade-runners, 116; organizes blockade-running, 120

Harman, Maj. John, chief quartermaster to Stonewall Jackson, 83
Holmes, Gen. Theophilus H., C.S.A., 31, 32, 52, 53
Hood, Gen. John B., C.S.A., 35–36, 37; Tennessee Campaign of, 86
Horses, 103–106; for Confederate Army, 90; supply of in Confederacy, 93; a factor in Confederate logistics, 103–106

INDEX